Skipton 2000

The Millennium Walk

compiled by Ian Lockwood

This first edition published December 1999

Dedicated to:
The people who make Skipton special

Limited First Edition of 2000

December 1999

30 colour photographs, one sketch map, one drawing
Illustrations editor Geoff Thomas

Published by
THE SKIPTON MILLENNIUM TASK FORCE
36 Sheep Street, Skipton, North Yorkshire BD23 1HY
E-mail: book@thomas-skipton.co.uk
01756 795353

© Ian Lockwood and Geoff Thomas

ISBN 0 9537484 0 5   hard back
ISBN 0 9537484 1 3   leather bound
ISBN 0 9537484 2 1   soft cover

Printed by
Lamberts Print & Design, Station Road, Settle, North Yorkshire BD24 9AA
01729 822177

Contents

	Preface	v
Chapter 1	The High Street	1
Chapter 2	The Castle	17
Chapter 3	Holy Trinity	22
Chapter 4	Mill Bridge	29
Chapter 5	Water Street and the canal	35
Chapter 6	Ermysted's	45
Chapter 7	Workhouse and hospital	57
Chapter 8	Mills and textiles	61
Chapter 9	Railways	67
Chapter 10	Riots	74
Chapter 11	Caroline Square	82
Chapter 12	Newmarket Street	88
Chapter 13	Shortbank Road	95
Chapter 14	Elementary schools	99
Chapter 15	Otley Street	107
Appendix 1	The Guy Fawkes Riot	116
Appendix 2	School Life in Skipton	121
Appendix 3	Some notable Skiptonians	131
Appendix 4	High Street shops	146

Skipton 2000

Preface

THIS book came about almost by accident. It was early in 1998 that the then mayor of Skipton, Pam Heseltine, called a public meeting to discuss what Skipton was going to do to celebrate the new millennium. A number of citizens turned out and there were a few ideas put forward but even at that early stage there was one big question – who was going to do the work and finance it? The meeting decided that a group should be formed to take it forward and so Pam Heseltine, Ian Lockwood, editor of the Craven Herald, Rev Adrian Botwright, rector of Skipton, Derek Evans, of Skipton Lions, David Buckroyd, headmaster of Ermysted's Grammar School, Ann Marshall, representing Skipton Chamber of Trade and Geoff Thomas, owner of Thomas's Jewellers in Sheep Street, found themselves, somewhat reluctantly, voted on to a body to take the matter further. We also had valuable initial input from Coun Robert Heseltine, county and district councillor as we found our feet.

At our first meeting Geoff Thomas, a self-confessed chatterer! was made chairman and we pondered over a number of suggestions, some of them our own, some of them put to us by townsfolk. Soon it became apparent that many of the ideas were not workable, required planning permission that was unlikely to be forthcoming or would require finance and it was obvious that rather than a body to actually do something, we would be a body to encourage, prod, cajole and co-ordinate matters. I cannot remember who it was who first suggested a Millennium Walk round Skipton taking in the social and economic history of the town, but it was something that we latched on to. The walk already existed, it just needed putting together.

Setting the route was comparatively easy. We were keen to include as many interesting aspects of the town as possible while also making a pleasant stroll taking in the views. Skipton is much loved by visitors across the world and has more than its share of pleasing sights. The canal and High Street were obvious candidates but it was also decided to take in other aspects, such as the railway station and Wilderness, which might be overlooked by the visitor and whose stories are not known by many Skiptonians. Having declared our intentions through the Craven Herald, we set about making our walk become a reality. There were parts of the walk which were difficult to follow, or impossible for the handicapped to access and this caused much soul searching. We had made an early decision that we did not want to be a financial body, raising or distributing funds so we held meetings with Craven District Council to see what could be done to help parts of the walk. In particular we were worried about narrow bridges across Eller Beck on the Springs Canal and wanted a route on to Gargrave Road from the Coach Street car park. Our initial conclusion from that discussion was one of gloom. The council made supportive noises, but promised nothing. Indeed, when finance was mentioned there was much obfuscation. Yet, behind the scenes something was clearly happening and the council was listening. Some months later, and to our pleasant surprise, the council was to announce a partnership with British Waterways, Craven Counts (a partnership involving the council and local businesses) and Skipton Building Society to carry out £250,000 worth of improvements to the towpaths. In a separate project they were also to refurbish the Coach Street car park and, to our delight, included steps and a ramp up from the car park on to Gargrave Road, thus removing a small but annoying detour. Also falling into place behind the scenes was the acquisition by Skipton Civic Society from Whitbread's Brewery of the Wilderness. Gwynne Walters of the Civic Society worked extremely hard ensuring that this section of the walk was improved, thus completing another link in the chain. British Waterways found the where-with-all to complete projects on Springs Canal after a final bout of local funding. The Rotary Club of Skipton gave a promise of £3,000 for signs and Jim Wales came up with the design for waymarkers along the route.

It also became apparent that a guide book was needed. While the need for a basic route map with points of interest was obvious, we became enthused about the stories and fables which Skiptonians were telling us about the walk. One problem was that over the years half truths and misconceptions had become firmly etched on the public mind and, when challenged, there was little if any evidence for the "facts". For example, there are still fables of a secret passageway between Skipton Castle and various destinations such as the Black Horse, the Red Lion, or even Bolton Abbey. No-one had ever found such a subterranean passage and the story can be dismissed as an old wife's tale. Similarly, the account of Roundhead soldiers being poisoned at the Black Horse during the Civil War siege of Skipton Castle is a nice story, but nowhere documented – other than the modern plaque on the wall of the pub. Even so, there was plenty of fascinating material and so it was decided to provide a more detailed book, based upon the walk and that duty fell upon myself.

Co-incidentally, papers had come into my possession from William Harbutt Dawson, editor of the History of Skipton published in 1882. In some ways I felt a link with Dawson, who was a former editor of the Pioneer, which was to merge with the Herald many years later. His father was editor-proprietor of the Pioneer and Dawson was a mere 22 years old when he published his History of Skipton. It has been ruthlessly plundered by many subsequent guide book authors and the town owes him a huge debt for his meticulous and extensive research. Dawson moved south and in 1940, when in his 80s, he revisited his original work, updated it and sold the copyright to the Craven Herald with a view to them publishing it. Alas, he was not to live to see his work re-published. The Herald wrote to Dawson, and later his widow, pointing out that rationing of paper during and then after the war prevented the revised work being printed. It was to be 1972, with Dawson long dead, when the Herald got round to republishing a second edition of his opus! The papers were handwritten notes updating and altering (often on minor points of style) his earlier work though few of these changes were incorporated into that later edition. Dawson's handwriting proved almost impenetrable to me at first but I gradually became used to his ways and, when the going got tough, it seemed as though there was a personal link across the decades to inspire me on.

Dawson, however, was not perfect. It is astonishing that he dismissed the coming of the canal and railway to Skipton in a sentence or two even though these were events of massive significance to the development of the town. Perhaps the reason is contained within his preface to the 1882 book: "My aim has been to avoid repetition of matter already well known". Another problem was that many facts and buildings are taken as common knowledge. While the readers of 1882 might have known full well where Mr So-and-so's was, more than a century on there was considerable detective work involved. To try to ensure future readers, I have included at the end a list of occupants of the High

Street area as of December 1999.

It is now appropriate to mention the modern day sources who have helped in the production of this book. Roger Pyrah performed invaluable groundwork finding out facts and figures to provide a basis for research. He also responded with good humour to demands for clarification or more information. Roger assembled many of the basic facts and it would be fair to say that he built the foundations on which the book is constructed.

Much of the work on the railway is taken from Kenneth Jackson's series of articles published by the Craven Herald to mark the 150th anniversary of the opening of the railway in 1997. The forthright story of Ermysted's history draws heavily from AM Gibbon's history while the recent book by Stephanie Carter and Alexandra Weatherhead is the best source for the history of the college.

The late Dr Geoffrey Rowley took Dawson a stage further. His meticulous research into the buildings and history of Skipton was an essential reference point and I must acknowledge my debt to his work in pointing the way forward. Others have also offered guidance and constructive criticism to varying degrees – Valentine Rowley, Jean Myers, Mary Wales, Judith Addyman, Don Howard, Donald Moorby, Bob Hannam, Siobhan Kirrane at the Craven Museum and staff at the Craven Library for their pleasantness in dealing with my many technical problems with microfilm. Tony Harman of Maple Leaf Images provided some of the pictures and lent Geoff a camera! Cheryl Singhals of the Cresap Society of America provided details of the life of Thomas Cresap. I claim the author's usual plea for forgiveness should I have forgotten anyone who has had an input, no matter how small, and been overlooked.

With their help and my own research the book evolved. Writing a guide book and a history combined is an unusual approach to take and not without its problems. At points it would have been appropriate to link incidents or buildings together in the text but the geography of the walk dictated that they had to be separate. I have attempted to make the narrative as logical as possible but should the reader be exasperated, then I crave their indulgence.

It was not my intention to rehash some of the perhaps dry and dull facts about the buildings. Instead I attempted to put forward the human side of the development of the town. For instance, the history of Holy Trinity's stones, mortar and monuments is well documented and I could have added little. But on delving deeper, it became clear that many of the facts were fascinating and little known. Corrupt vicars, drunken churchwardens, rotting flesh from corpses buried under flagstones in the vaults mixing with new gas lighting causing some people to pass out – how could I miss out such details!

It also became apparent that there were stories which did not fit comfortably into any part of the walk but were too tasty for my journalistic instincts to omit! I have incorporated them into a series of appendices. I also found a number of characters of whom wonderful anecdotes abound and thus they are woven into the story as part of the fabric of Skipton's community. Thus Billy Gelling appears in the appendix. Doubtless he would be surprised to find himself recorded for posterity but any Skiptonian born and bred in the town in the first half of the century would know the name and the reputation! I would have been keen to include the story of more notable Skiptonians but alas time crept up on me and it was imperative to have the book published in time for the Millennium!

So the book came to life. Several people have had an input, made suggestions, criticisms and additions. Some advice has been incorporated, some has not. No book can be written by committee and may I plead the editor's prerogative of having the final say. It is not, however, my book, nor that of the Skipton Millennium Task Force. We are proud that it has cost not a penny to the town, that all profits will go back to the town and that the copyright reverts to the town. The Millennium Task Force will not survive the first year of the new millennium. It is for future generations to preserve and protect the Millennium Walk and to update this book.

Ian Lockwood, Skipton, December 1999.

Skipton 2000

Original design of Waymarker by Jim Wales

Front Cover: Skipton Castle and Holy Trinity
Back Cover: Springs Canal and Pocket Park

1: The High Street

The Millennium Walk starts on the High Street, outside Barclays Bank

SKIPTON is renowned far and wide as a pleasant, interesting town. Visitors flock in to explore its backways, peruse its shops and market and stroll along the canalside. Close enough to the metropolitan centres to be an easy drive, it also profits from its boast of being the Gateway to the Dales. The Millennium Walk will, hopefully, underline the town's status as a tourist centre and also shed light on its history. But while most people take great delight in the town, its buildings, its surroundings and its attractions of castle, church and canal, it was not always considered to be such a pleasant spot. Indeed, before trains and charabancs made day excursions out of the smoky, industrial sprawls of the West Riding and East Lancashire a welcome treat, Skipton was often derided as a backward place. Forgive me if I open this account of the town with some less than flattering descriptions from the past.

In 1792 the Hon John Byng, compiling a diary of his journeys across the country came upon Skipton and was moved to describe it as: "this nasty, filthily inhabited town; for I never saw more slatterns or dirtier houses". The castle was: "a most inconvenient, miserable, tattered place, with neither beauty of building nor pleasing antiquity but a melancholy wretchedness of bad old rooms, some miserable tapestries and some basely neglected pictures."

The Gentleman's Magazine of 1794 concurred. Skipton was "thinly peopled, where trade has not yet spread affluence nor the arts of civilisation polished the general manners or enlarged the sentiments of the inhabitants"

Frederick Montague, in his book Gleanings in Craven wrote: "As a place of business and trade to any great extent it is unimportant. Though it possesses local advantages inferior to no town in the United Kingdom, but I have always observed that where, as in the present instance, a town is under the domination of a few individuals who only require their rents to be transmitted to their bankers with regularity and whose interest ceases with their lives, there is neither desire or ambition evinced in the prosperity of the place."

William Ranger, inspector for the Board of Health, 1857 wrote a damning report on the town's sanitary condition and reached the conclusion: "the criminals of our land had seven times as much space allotted to them as some of the poor of Skipton have. The prisons were cleaner, sweeter and purer than some of the dwellings he had visited."

Major Cookson, writing in 1859, put his finger on the cause: the refusal of the Tufton family, owners of the castle and most of the land around, to open up land for development: "The town has no room to expand; the castle people will not sell the fields around it on any building terms. Skipton has one broad street and several alleys, a ruinous old castle with a keep, three cotton mills and looks at a standstill."

Today, opinions are far more complimentary. High Street, wide and busy, is almost impassable on market day in spring and summer as visitors flock in to take advantage of the market. The width of the High Street came as a result of the town's markets. Farmers poured in from the Dales to sell their produce. Early photographs show cattle thronging the streets and casual labourers, many of them Irish were hired at the setts for hay making. Cattle fairs were originally held on alternate Tuesdays but in the 19th century they were held on alternate Mondays. There was also a pig market and, in autumn, an annual horse fair which again drew in crowds from all over the region. It was, by all accounts, a most unpleasant atmosphere for all.

William Harbutt Dawson, author of Skipton's definitive history, witnessed the cattle market in action on the High Street as editor of the Craven Pioneer. Many years later he was to write: "Ancient though that market was, it will be difficult for future generations to understand how an anachronism so dangerous to public health and opposed to public convenience should have been tolerated so long. It is not exaggeration to say that for one day in every fortnight all citizens to whom filth, evil odours, noise, bad language and cruelty to dumb animals were obnoxious had a sort of informal injunction to stay within their houses all day long unless duty dictated otherwise.

The tradesmen had always been divided in their opinions as to whether the street market was especially advantageous to them or the reverse and no blame attached to them for its continuance, but the inhabitants generally regarded it as an unmitigated nuisance. It was only a last warning, however, given in 1884 to the Local Board of Health by the supreme health authority in London that, unless the market was at once abolished from the streets and transferred to a suitable position elsewhere, it would be closed altogether which led to action being taken."

That suitable position was in Broughton Road, where, in 1886, Messers Throup and Davis opened an auction mart near the railway station in order to try and reduce the number of sheep and cattle and the mess in the High Street. Even so, the cattle markets continued to be held in the High Street until 1906.

A regular feature at hay making time was the arrival of Irish labourers on the High Street offering themselves as casual workers to local farmers, a practice which survived until shortly after the Second World War. The Craven Herald reported in 1947 that the Irish workers were asking prices of between £35 and £40 a month on top of board and lodgings while before the war the going rate had been six or seven pounds.

In 1906 a cattle market was created behind the Town hall at a cost of £4,000. It incorporated Jerry Croft and part of the home croft of the Red Lion Inn. Rope Walk, which ran parallel to Otley Street from what is now Rackham's car park, was also incorporated into the new cattle market. At long last the streets of Skipton were free from sheep and cattle and the resulting mess. Just before the outbreak of the Second World War, the Cattle Market behind the Town Hall was closed and all livestock went to the Broughton Road site. During the war the War Office commandeered the land behind the Town Hall. Older Skiptonians remember tanks and other military equipment gathered there. When the war ended, the land became a car park, a purpose it still serves today. Later the auction mart was moved once again, in 1990, when a new building was opened on the outskirts of the town, on the Gargrave road, alongside the bypass. The old site became Morrison's supermarket, the shape of whose foyer reflects the shape of the old auction ring.

While the market was central to Skipton's growth and prosperity yet, very much like today, it was not fondly regarded by many townsfolk. While today there are those who argue that the stalls of the contemporary market clogs up the town and stifles trade, back in the early days of the century there was considerable pressure to move the market. Much of this came from businessmen unconnected with the trade of sheep and cattle who found picking their way among the dung far from pleasant. The pubs also were a source of some irritation and when the market was moved behind the Town Hall, there was clearly some reckoning from the sober-minded sections of the community. The end of High Street cattle markets provided the licensing bench with the excuse to refuse to renew licenses.

Today the motor car is king of the High Street, with motorists scrambling for vacant spots on the setts, a scene which would have amazed the town 100 years ago. The very first car spotted in the town went through on April 18 1897 and was owned by the town's MP Walter Morrison who lived at Tarn House, Malham. He welcomed many visitors such as Charles Kingsley, who used his stay there as the inspiration for his book the Water Babies, with Walter Morrison fitting into the role of the squire. He drove through on the Friday and returned on the Sunday, causing "considerable interest" according to the Herald.

RN Myers possessed the first motor vehicle in Skipton, a wagon used for collecting wool from the farmers up the dales. The firm was the last wool merchants in Skipton, a town where fortunes were made on the back of the wool trade. Operating from a warehouse off Coach Street, the firm collected fleeces from farmers all over the Dales, right up to Sedbergh but in the Second World War the industry was nationalised under the British Wool Marketing Board and it remains under Government control.

The lime trees lining the street were planted in 1897 to mark the Diamond Jubilee of Queen Victoria. Despite being bumped by cars, knocked by market stalls and festooned with lights at Christmas, they are still going surviving today! These lime trees (lindens) are in fact totally unsuitable trees for the High Street - they are susceptible to pollution and fared poorly with the arrival, in the year of their planting, of the motor vehicles, hence their stunted forms, and they deposit a black sticky mess from the leaves coating stalls, cars and setts. They just happened to be fashionable in the late Victorian times.

The High Street was the scene of a notable event in Skipton's social history, the Guy Fawkes Riot of November 5-6 1872. Skipton, it seems, was an enthusiastic supporter of Bonfire Night celebrations, an excuse for the townsfolk to let their hair down. It was one of the few days in which the church bells were rung all day at the expense of the parish (in 1744 the ringers' pay was revised and the churchwardens resolved that in future they should have "five shillings and no more for ringing upon extraordinary days except the fifth of November, for which they are to have seven shillings". Indeed, there is evidence that the town paid for bonfires to be built).

Into this scene of general festivities stepped a new superintendent of police, Thomas Grisdale, who appears to have been somewhat officious. In 1871 he showed signs of disapproval and in 1872 appears to have resolved to have clamped down on the celebrations which may have got out of hand (Dawson described "innocuous pistol firing"). Whatever the case, the killjoy stepped in posting notices around the town warning against unruly behaviour and prohibiting the setting off fireworks, a measure which was none too popular with locals used to some serious celebrations.

The superintendent had made sure that there was a large body of police to back up his warnings and, no doubt as the beer set in, the mood of the locals grew ever more resentful. The main street was busier than before and the time-honoured custom of discharging fireworks and firearms began with increased enthusiasm. As the night progressed, there were repeated attacks by the police, which were met with increased resentment. Dawson records the police charging without discrimination and in return being roughly handled – all to the accompaniment of brass bands wandering round the streets. Truncheon blows injured townsfolk and policemen too suffered wounds from sticks and stones, including the superintendent.

The following night nearly 100 constables were on duty but the night passed off quietly. It was, if anything, a moral victory for Skiptonians. The zealous superintendent was soon afterwards removed to another part of the county and it seems a note of defiance was struck as Skipton schoolboys were recorded as chanting "Gunpowder Plot shall never be forgot as long as Skipton stands on a rock". Perhaps in the long run Superintendent Grisdale was the victor. There are no further accounts of fireworks in the High Street. (A fuller account of the Riot is given in appendix one on page 124).

We set off on the Millennium Walk by crossing High Street at the pedestrian crossing and turn right, towards the top of High Street, dominated by Holy Trinity Church.

At the northern end of Middle Row is the shop Jumpers, but many still refer to it nostalgically as Manby's Corner, after the ironmonger's shop which stood here for many years. The front of the building was of much admired mahogany (now painted over) and was installed by Walter Shuttleworth, who also designed the staircase in Craven College – he was later to become a teacher at Ermysted's. The clock set into the gable end is dated May 20 1912 and was one of the first illuminated clocks in the country. Alas is has not worked for some years although there are hopes that the dawn of a new Millennium will alter that state of affairs.

Originally all properties on the west side of the High Street would have had long gardens extending from them. In the early 1800s, as Skipton developed as an industrial centre, these disappeared, to be replaced by narrow passageways, known locally as ginnels, leading to in-fill buildings. Some guide books (and indeed locals) may tell you that these narrow passageways were built to be easily defended against the Scots. Alas the story is rubbish; the much-maligned Scots were never that frequent visitors and these ginnels are a much later development, more a product of trying to cram as many people as possible into as small an area as possible. They also had the added benefit of being narrow enough to prevent beasts intruding down them on market days. These ginnels still exist today, openings off the High Street which the visitor to the town may be unwilling to explore. These ginnels housed the majority of Skipton residents until the town expanded outwards but conditions were cramped and distinctly unsanitary. Many of these houses still existed until after World War Two, often without running water, but a massive slum clearance programme took place. Now the ginnels lead on to a conservation area. Some of the original housing remains, in other parts new housing and shops have been sympathetically developed to replicate the original style.

On the opposite side of the road is Boot's the Chemist. Every town it seems has its Boots. Skipton's moved here in 1975 from further down Sheep Street. Before that it was a famous Skipton store, GH Mason's, plumbers, painters and decorators who moved to this site in 1875. Before that a corn dealer had occupied the premises, handy for dealing with the farmers who came to the aforementioned market. Mason's just failed to see their centenary here, closing in

August 1974 with the chemists moving in a few months later.

The current Yorkshire Bank building replaced one of the Skipton pubs which closed with the demise of the High Street cattle market, the Bay Horse. The Yorkshire Penny Bank opened in September 1898. Outside the old inn was the ring to which were tied bulls for baiting. This old practice seems particularly cruel to the modern mind, particularly as it was seen as a sport. The bull was tethered to a ring by a rope and bets were struck as to the performance of the dogs. The practice was finally made illegal in 1835. However, there appears to have been more than a sporting reason for this cruel practice judging from records of court proceedings. A typical example from the court leet records is from 1738: "Whereas Robert Heelis and Robert Johnson, clerks of the market for the burg of Skipton, have presented unto us that Peter Moorby, a butcher within this burg hath killed and sold within the burg aforesaid a bull without baiting, we the jury do amerce (i.e. fine) the said Moorby for so doing the sum of six shillings and eight pence." This is by no means the sole example and it is thought that the torment and pain of being attacked by dogs and stabbed with sharp darts made the adrenaline flow and so, it was believed, tenderised the meat. The practice became a public spectacle and ritual and woe betide the farmer who sold his flesh unbaited.

A plaque on the walls of the Yorkshire Bank commemorates this practice and, close inspection will reveal a stone in the sett still with its ring intact – alas the chances of seeing it are slim as the stone is almost certain to be covered by either market stall or parked car! However, it seems as though this ring is a later addition long after the practice ceased for, writing in 1882, Dawson comments that the ring was removed because of the inconvenience it caused.

Further down High Street are the premises of the Craven Herald – The 'Voice of the Dales' which was first produced on this site in 1853. Until early 1998 the Herald ran a shop but a refurbishment led to the leasing of the shop to Thornton's chocolates, with entrance to the newspaper located down a 'ginnel' and its offices above the shop. The newspaper owes its origins to an enterprising printer, Robert Tasker, who produced his first newspaper from the shop. It was a monthly publication, crown folio size (slightly larger than standard typing paper) selling around 700 copies. In 1857 it was enlarged to broadsheet size but only five editions were printed as Tasker had taken over as the town's postmaster and was barred from printing a newspaper.

Another newspaper, the West Riding Pioneer had been founded in 1857 and its office was in Middle Row, on the site of the current Nat West bank. The Pioneer was strongly pro-Liberal in character. The Conservatives in the district, anguished at being denied a political voice, hit back and founded the Craven Conservative Newspaper Company Limited with the specific aim of providing a counterbalance. In July 1874 they acquired Robert Tasker's premises from his son, James (who had still carried on as printers and stationers) and revived the Craven Herald. In 1937 the two newspapers merged, forming the Craven Herald and Pioneer, which printed from a press housed at the rear of the premises. By 1988 that press, built in the days of Queen Victoria, was well past its sell-by-date and major investment was required for replacement. The newspaper was sold to the Westminster Press group (now Newsquest) and printed in Bradford. However, the reporters continued to operate from offices overlooking the High Street and today the Craven Herald sells some 19,500 copies a week. It is one of only three newspapers in the whole of the United Kingdom to still carry adverts only on its front page.

The newspaper industry, intending to mark the Millennium selected 50 all time classic pages for an exhibition. Among pages such as the Times' report on the Death of Nelson, the Daily Express's first man on the moon and the Daily Mirror's End of World War Two was a Herald front page of September 1999. It was the only weekly newspaper selected. The Herald's quaint ways endear it to locals. A famous misprint was the advert for a secretary good with figures to work for a "bust accountant" – it should have been a "busy accountant"!

The large bevelled shop windows were installed in 1912 and are now listed.

Next door to the Herald is Next shop (the only four storey building on the High Street). Just before the war this was Laycock's Antiques and an occasional visitor was Queen Mary, grandmother of our current Queen Elizabeth, popping in during her stays at the Duke of Devonshire's estates.

A little further along lies Skipton library and Craven College. Now providing education for more than 2,000, the college plays an important role in the educational life of the town. It is one of the lowest funded yet fastest growing colleges in the country, suffering from being somewhat cramped premises, which has forced it to establish its courses on several sites.

Its origins came from the Mechanics' Institute movement, educational societies to provide lectures and enlightenment so typical of the Victorian ethos of self-improvement. The origins of the Mechanics' Institute in Skipton are unclear but a recent history of the college (by Stephanie Carter and Alexandra

Woodhead) quotes figures of 100 members and a library of 250 volumes when it joined the Yorkshire Union of Mechanics Institutes in 1845. Early meetings were held in a small room behind the Hole in the Wall pub in the High Street. The subjects studied were writing, arithmetic, grammar and Latin. It appears to have closed for two years to be reformed in 1847 under the presidency of Henry Alcock, the Skipton solicitor whose name crops up regularly in the history of the town. During this mid-century period it was offering lectures such as The Elements of Design, Nineveh and Ancient Art, The Poetry of the Pope era. Premises were always a problem and classes were held in the Wesleyan Schoolroom in Millfields the Temperance Hall in Sackville Street, the Old Town Hall in Sheep Street and the British School in Otley Street.

This problem of a permanent home appears to have galvanised leading citizens of the town into action and it was perceived that an ideal way for the town to mark Queen Victoria's 50 years on the throne in 1887 would be the provision of a permanent building with library, newsroom, conversation room, lecture theatre and classrooms. A sub-committee was formed to bring the project to fruition and the site on High Street was chosen, the land being purchased from the Castle for a fee of £1,500. Among the contributors to a fund were mill owner John Bonny Dewhurst (a member of the committee) who gave £500, Lord Hothfield of the Castle, who gave £300, brewer John Scott, who gave £200 and £100 each from the Duke of Devonshire, Walter Morrison and Mathew Wilson.

The first college building, known as the Skipton Science and Arts School, was thus erected on land behind Birdsall's jewellers and Wildman's furniture shop at this point on the High Street and opened on September 25 1894 in a special ceremony. Fund raising continued and the shops were removed in 1908 to make way for the second phase of the project, completed on February 19 1910 when the new frontage for the library was opened with the help of a £3,000 grant from the Carnegie Trust (marked by a plaque on the front of the building. The Trust also funded other libraries in the area, such as the one in Clitheroe). The grandiose frontage of this building did not please everyone however, and the famous architect Sir Nikolaus Pevsner in his book the Buildings of England in 1981 described it as "the only building that runs counter to this modest street... too high, too townish".

The original building, behind the library and main entrance, consisted of a large rectangular block, three storeys high with a basement and is little changed today. The success of the college can be gauged by its growth. The history, published in 1999, puts its register at 680 full time and 5,600 part time students with 56 salaried academic staff (14 fractional appointments, 210 part time lecturers, 85 business support staff (23 part of them part time) and 21 manual staff (15 part time). Current college principal Alan Blackwell is quoted as saying: "Craven College has built up an enviable reputation for quality which has been endorsed by the college's inspection from the Further Education Funding Council. In terms of its achievement rates and progression into work the college goes from strength to strength. Our learning environment has been the platform for thousands of people to successfully launch or relaunch their careers".

Outside the library stands the statue of Sir Mathew Wilson, whose claim to fame is that he was the first MP for the Skipton Division. Alas this fine town has not produced many notable sons and perhaps the fact that its first MP has such an impressive statue is a sign of this. Perhaps the most famous Skiptonian of the modern era was Iain Macleod, a Conservative Chancellor of the Exchequer and a man tipped for leadership of the Conservative Party before his early death. He was found dead in his 11 Downing Street home, victim of a heart attack. He was the son of a doctor in the town, living in Keighley Road in premises now occupied by the solicitors JP Mewies and Co.

But back to our first MP, elected for the new Skipton constituency in 1885 after previously representing Clitheroe and the West Riding Northern Division. His hold on Skipton did not last long as in 1886 he was narrowly defeated, along with Gladstone's Government, with Unionist candidate Walter Morrison taking the seat. The statue was the result of a meeting of prominent Liberals, including John Bonny Dewhurst, who wished to mark his lifelong service to the Liberal cause. The Pioneer was enthusiastic; the Conservative-leaning Herald highly unimpressed. It poured scorn on the statue, stating it was "in recognition of his Parliamentary services, services which consisted of blindly following the behests of Mr Gladstone changing as the latter changed and swearing if he swore that white was black and black white."

Funds were raised mostly from the Bradford business community and there was much bitterness about locating the statue in the main road, at the top of the High Street with allegations that the Local Board of Health was not properly consulted. It was unveiled on June 6 1888, by the Marquess of Ripon and Sir Mathew Wilson was there to witness the event (a rare occurrence, few have had a statue put up to them in their own lifetime – he was to live until 1914). The Pioneer said that "Skipton has undoubtedly been ennobled by a beautiful ornament, by a work of art which would grace any public street or square in the land." The Herald, of course, disagreed. "The likeness of the old gentleman is passable but he is perched on a block which much resembles a gravestone". It dubbed the edifice the Consolation Statue, deeming it a consolation to Sir Mathew for being kicked out of his seat by Skipton voters.

Made out of bronze by Bruce Jay it was unveiled to the public not in the place it stands now but at a position of greater prominence, at the top of the High Street. The end of the First World War sealed his fate as it was decided that a memorial to the fallen of the town were more worthy of such an eminent site and Sir Mathew was moved to his present slot in June 1921. The story is that when moved Sir Mathew wobbled until an enterprising engineer slotted a penny under his left foot but this story is more likely to be a myth.

In 1974 poor Sir Mathew was threatened with another ignominious fate – removal from the High Street altogether to Aireville Park in order to create "more space". However, the move was defeated on the grounds that the site vacated by Sir Mathew would only be taken up by a market stall.

Before leaving Skipton's first MP, it is worth recording the memories of Dawson, writing in 1946 and then in his 80s, of his childhood recollections of polling in Skipton. Voters, and in 1884 there were only 414 eligible in the town, cast their vote not in secret but in the full publicity of the street by mounting a simple wooden stage about four feet high known as the hustings "somewhat similar to the portable platform of the predatory quack doctors and 'cheap Jack' auctioneers who used to scour the countryside in search of silly victims". The voter mounted the stage to declare his vote while a raucous crowd, well lubricated with ale, watched the proceedings and groaned or cheered depending upon the political sentiments expressed.

Further up the High Street lies the Black Horse, which dates back to 1676 although a pub existed on this site at least 30 years previously but this is not the oldest pub in Skipton. That honour belongs to the Red Lion, which lies across the road and has been a license premises for more than 500 years. Workmen redecorating the Red Lion in the early 1990s stripped back some plaster to discover a 400 year old large arched fireplace and chimney which is on view today. The Red Lion has also large arched cellars. Some accounts state that the Red Lion started life as a hospital of St Mary Magdalene, which was for the support

Skipton 2000

of lepers. Leprosy was not uncommon in the early Middle Ages but the disease had largely died out by the time the Black Death arrived in England in 1349. However, there is a strong opinion that it is unlikely that a leper hospital would be situated within the centre of the settlement, so close to the castle, the normal siting being away from the inhabited areas. Like most inns in Skipton, the Red Lion was a combined farmhouse. Jerry Croft, part of the Red Lion farm, was taken over when the cattle market was constructed behind the Town Hall in 1906. The Red Lion farm ceased after the First World War.

But back to the Black Horse. On the front of the building is a badge with the date 1676 and the initial 'G' together with symbols of the butcher's trade. This probably denotes Robert Goodgeon, a butcher, who built this house after he acquired the property in 1676. Until 1706 the pub was known as the King's Head and there is a tradition that this site housed the mews of Richard Duke of Gloucester, later King Richard III, when he was Lord of the Honour of Skipton. Richard III's reputation as the murderous king owes much to Shakespeare but he became Lord of Skipton after a deed equally as dastardly carried out by the Cliffords who owned the Castle and lands of Skipton. The Cliffords had been supporters of the Lancastrian cause when the War of the Roses broke out and at the Battle of St Albans in 1455 Thomas Clifford was killed facing the Yorkist forces led by the Duke of York. His son, John Clifford, was equally as staunch a Lancastrian and in 1460 he led part of the Lancastrian forces which inflicted defeat on a smaller Yorkist force at Sandal, killing the Duke of York. After the battle, on the bridge at Sandal, the Duke's young son, the Earl of Rutland, a mere boy was captured and stabbed to death by Clifford with the words "thy father slew mine and so will I thee.". The scene is captured in Shakespeare's Henry VI. It was not the only act of barbarity carried out by Clifford, who returned to the field of battle, sought out the corpse of the Duke of York and hacked off the head, which he mounted on a pole and placed on the gates of the city York

Three months later Clifford was dead, one of many Lancastrians slaughtered in an overwhelming victory for the Yorkist faction at Towton, near Tadcaster - although he died in a skirmish before the battle, shot in the throat by an archer waiting in ambush. After Towton the Clifford estates were confiscated and granted to Sir William Stanley and, upon his death in 1471, to Richard Duke of Gloucester. Legend has it that the Duke visited his Skipton possessions. Outside the pub today there is still a block of three stone steps used when mounting a horse which is supposed to have been used by Richard himself. The Duke of course, became King Richard III and was given an evil reputation by Shakespeare but he was much loved in the north for being a benefactor to the area. He gave a gift of £20 to Holy Trinity Church when it was extended eastwards.

Another tale of the Black Horse is that during the Civil War, when Skipton Castle was besieged by Parliamentarian forces, a troop of soldiers arrived at the inn and were served with poisoned ale, although this appears to owe more to a past landlord's fertile imagination than to any documented evidence. The Black Horse was an old coaching inn on the main Leeds to Kendal turnpike road and as recently as 1906 it was advertising post horses and conveyances. The present ballroom was built in the late 1930s and provided alternative, and larger, premises to the Devonshire Hotel in Newmarket Street. The ballroom was also large enough to provide temporary billets for troops during the Second World War and when they left a children's party was held to mark the end of the war – but only after the floor had been thoroughly scrubbed. In 1998 there was a major refurbishment of the inside and a pleasant area overlooking the canal at the rear was constructed.

David Goldie's shop at 4 High Street is a pleasing addition to the town. This was a doctor's surgery, with Dr Forsyth Wilson practising here from 1877 to 1886. Here his son, Charles MacMoran Wilson, later Lord Moran was born. Lord Moran's claim to fame is that he was Winston Churchill's physician. Dr Wilson was succeeded by Dr Russell and the house later became known to Skiptonians as Dinsdale's, selling quality leather goods.

At the Black Horse take care in crossing the busy High Street to the Town Hall opposite.

Across the road lies Skipton Town Hall, built in 1862 by a private concern, the Skipton Public Buildings Company, at a cost of £4,500 on the site of the old vicarage. The Town Hall was built in classical style with columns and pediments and once boasted an ornate canopy which alas was taken down when rust set in. The Town Hall balcony was used to make important announcements – such as the result of an election – but this practice has, alas, long since fallen into abeyance. In 1878 the large hall was enlarged and its height increased. In 1895 the Town Hall was purchased by Skipton Urban District Council for

£4,500 from the private company and continues to be the main centre of entertainment for the town. The Friends of Skipton Hospital have been holding bingo sessions there on Tuesday evenings for more than 50 years and it is a regular home to bazaars, exhibitions and the occasional theatrical or musical production. The works of the Skipton Amateur Operatic Society are particularly well patronised - much more so than the unfortunate Bradford-based Q20 Theatre Company who, on December 1 1971 raised the curtain on their production America Hurrah to find just one person in the audience – Annie Hyde, of Park Street.

It is worth entering here to visit the Craven Museum. It owes its origins to three local groups, the Mechanics Institute, the Craven Scientific and Naturalists Association and the Adult School (a Quaker education group) with Dr Arthur Raistrick playing a key role. A public meeting was held in the Town Hall and Mechanics gave the princely sum of £50 to get the project underway. The museum was a huge success from the start, acquiring items excavated from the Roman fort at Elslack and the Naturalists' collection of prehistoric finds from Elbolton Cave. It was originally sited in the library but the sheer size and value of the collections persuaded the committee that they ought to join with the local authority. In 1934 Skipton Urban Council took the museum under its wing and the librarian took on the role of curator. Many people today may remember the walls of caved birds and rows of old fashioned glass cases giving the impression of a cuckoo in the nest as the museum continued to growth, taking up much needed space and resources. In 1974 local government re-organisation caused the library and museum to be separated, the latter coming under the control of Craven District Council. It was moved across the High Street into new, purpose-built accommodation on the first floor of the Town Hall annexe, premises funded by Mrs Coulthurst. For the first time professional museum staff were employed to develop the service. Almost all the items in the museum were freely donated by local people and are now highly regarded. Admission is free and opening hours at the date of publication of this book are: April to September, Monday, Wednesday, Thursday and Friday 10am-5pm; Saturday 10am-12noon, 1pm-5pm; Sunday 2-5pm. October to March, Monday, Wednesday, Thursday, Friday 2-5pm; Saturday 10am-12 noon, 1pm-4pm. Closed all day Tuesday throughout the year.

On the first floor of the Town Hall is the council chamber. Here Skipton's first council met, Skipton Urban Council, formed the under Local Government

Act of 1895. In 1974 another bout of reorganisation took place and Skipton Urban Council was abolished, most of its powers being taken over by Craven District Council. A new authority, Skipton Town Council, with much lesser powers than the old Urban Council, was formed and still meets here. The ornate chairs and benches were crafted by the famous Robert Thompson, the Mouseman of Kildburn, whose trademark mouse can be spotted in the carvings.

From the Town Hall the route proceeds northwards for a few paces.

On a building to the side of the Town Hall is a plaque to Herbert Smith, who was actually from the village of Bradley, a couple of miles to the south of Skipton. He became an aircraft designer for the famous Sopwith firm. It was he who designed First World War aeroplanes such as the Sopwith Camel, which duelled in the skies above the Western Front. After the war Britain went into depression and Smith was enticed away to Japan – which had been a British ally during the war – and built up their military air force, to devastating effect as the attack on Pearl Harbour was to prove. It is intriguing to think that those aeroplanes and carriers, which so damaged the US Navy and brought the Americans into the war, were the developments of a Skipton man's designs. Smith had returned home some time before the start of the war but his skills were not called on, and his work for Japan sent him into something of a disgrace in the United Kingdom until he was finally recognised by the plaque in his home town.

In the centre of the roundabout at the top of the High Street is the cenotaph to Skipton's dead of the First World War (those who fell in the Second World War are commemorated in gate posts at an entrance to Aireville Park off Gargrave Road). The cenotaph was unveiled on April 22 1922 by the children of those in Skipton who had perished, requiring the removal of the aforementioned Sir Mathew Wilson. Earlier Sir Mathew had caused the removal from in front of the church gates of a gas lamp, dubbed "Old Gormless" reputedly because drunks, on their way home, would stagger into the lamp standard and address it as a "gormless thing".

A famous book, which still holds pride of place in many Craven households, was produced after the war, funded by Sir Walter Morrison, who owned the large house at Malham Tarn, and collated by the Craven Herald. The book, Craven's Part in the Great War, recorded those from Craven (which in those days included areas now administratively no longer part of the district, such Dent, Sedbergh, Barnoldswick and Earby) who perished. The book gives the name and origin of each Craven man who died in the war. There are several hundred names in the book, and even today, flicking through and seeing the images of men long forgotten who left these parts to give their lives for their country, is a poignant experience.

Leading across from the Town Hall to the gateway of Holy Trinity Church is a flagged path through the cobbled setts. Legend has it that these steps were put in by a vicar, whose home used to be on the site of the Town Hall. Fed up of trailing his cassock through the mud and other unmentionable deposits from the cattle marts on the setts he is supposed to have persuaded the churchwardens to finance a route over the cobbles and the beaten clay roadway. The account books of the churchwardens relate in May 1803 that it was resolved "that a proper causeway be made from the east side of High Street to the south entrance of the church gates and one on the west side of the same street..forming a junction at the church gates". No mention of the vicar's involvement is recorded.

Cross to the church gates and enter the churchyard. Look down the High Street at Mathew Wilson's view – follow the right hand path to the castle.

On the right the fine Georgian home now housing solicitors Walker Foster, erected in memory of George Annesley Fisher in 1957. The building was the property of the castle until 1956. In that year the castle was sold to the Fattorini estate and the house was sold to the solicitors. It was the home of Henry Alcock, himself a solicitor, who built Aireville Grange in 1856. It was the home of and surgery of a general practitioner, Dr Bob Fisher, until his death in 1937 and was then used by another doctor, John Goodall,

The road to the right is known as the Bailey and heads towards Knaresborough. In 1826, during a depression, the town authorities paid the poor sixpence a day to work at making a more gentle gradient of the hill by lowering the level of the road and adding the material to the raised walk, thus building the high retaining wall in place today. The Bailey was often referred to among townsfolk of the last century as Hard Times Walk .

Disabled persons should proceed carefully along the Bailey towards the Castle. Access is available to the Churchyard further on. But be aware that there are cobbles to traverse. Alternatively bear left and rejoin by the Catle pub at Mill Bridge.

2: The Castle

The Walk takes us to the very gateway of Skipton Castle, most of which is hidden behind the round towers and impressive gateway. This is in fact just an outer wall and a visit inside is highly recommended. It would add greatly to the time needed for the walk but to skip a visit to the castle would be to omit a great deal of Skipton's early history.

WHEN we walk up the High Street we are climbing the hill, the rocky outcrop which must have inspired Robert de Romille, a Norman warrior, to think in 1090 "what a good place for a castle". He would have seen the small hamlet of Sheeptown, then nestling slightly to the north and west of today's main thoroughfare. Looking down from the top of the 40 metre escarpment, seeing the beck, de Romille would have understood its strategic value as the hill faced north; Skipton, the frontier town against the Scots.

Visitors must enter through the gatehouse, the famous picture postcard scene of Skipton in many books, but in fact the original entrance was more to the north and west. This imposing gatehouse is in fact early 17th century, the work of the 5th earl of Cumberland, the "architect earl" as we might call him. He designed the grotto of shells in the present visitors' entrance on the right of the gatehouse as we enter. The 5th earl maintained the style of modernisation, the theme of redevelopment which can be found in the work of so many of the owners of the castle to the present day.

Through the gatehouse on the right is the domestic looking east wing. The whole wing was built in five months in about 1535 to accommodate the niece of Henry VIII, Lady Eleanor Brandon, on her marriage to Henry Clifford, later the 2nd earl of Cumberland, a somewhat extravagant wedding present! It was an arranged marriage that became a love match. On her death 10 years later the story goes that the earl fell down in total distress. He was believed to be dead and the servants laid out his body when one of them noticed he was still breathing. He was supposedly revived with the milk of a wet nurse!

The medieval castle can be found straight ahead. Its old entrance was turned 90 degrees and modernised, a remarkable show of confidence in the early Tudor era as it took away the main gates and the bridge. The medieval castle was a formidable obstacle. With rounded drum towers, curtain walls hanging between and a sloping skirt at the bottom. An attacker would have found it difficult, almost impossible to batter his way through the walls or cope with a barrage of rocks coming down from the skirt. The modern expression of skirting round a problem originates from this medieval warfare. There is also an archer's slit or murder hole, cut into the wall. Behind it the archer would have plenty of room to fire his arrow through the walls. The slot in the back of the ash-made arrow into which fitted the bow string was known as a 'nock' and at the start of the day, the archer 'nocked on' and when his day was done he 'nocked off', another expression to survive to the new millennium.

Turn right at the top of the steps and the visitor is in line with the original entrance, two main 1190 towers that formed the first stone castle. Entrance was not by a Robin Hood style drawbridge here with its slow movement and cumbersome windlass but a kind of see-saw! To get in visitors had to cross a bridge whose prop supports could easily and quickly be removed to allow the horizontal wooden floor to become a vertical gate. To the right was another small room housing a Norman fighting chamber, ready to deal with any attacker who got inside.

Inside is the famous yew tree in the Conduit Court, so called because a conduit bringing a supply of water to the castle terminates here. This lack of a spring within the keep itself was a disadvantage "as there would seldom want a traitor to reveal their course" and the garrison "were left to the chance of rain in this dripping climate and half an acre of leaden roofs to collect it". Water pipes bearing the date 1659, during the period of restoration after the civil war, can be seen here.

The castle came into the possession of the Clifford family in 1309, a gift of King Edward I for services rendered. Edward II stayed here in 1323.

Skipton during the civil war was a Royalist stronghold but was not under permanent siege, more of a strategic blockade. The surrender of Skipton Castle just before Christmas in 1645 marked the end of a long and honourable defence in the name of King Charles I. When hostilities commenced in 1642, Henry Clifford, Earl of Cumberland, was Lord Lieutenant of the county of York and it was his duty to execute the King's Commission. He held the castle for the king, although he was to die of natural causes during the Civil War and was buried in Holy Trinity. After an early skirmish in Tadcaster (during which Captain William Lister, of Thornton-in-Craven brother-in-law of the Parliamentarian Colonel Lambert, squire of Calton, Skipton, was killed) the castle was first besieged in December 1642 by a force of 300 men under the command of John Lambert.

For the first two years the siege was hardly vigorous, the object of the Parliamentary force being to prevent attacks by the garrison on Parliamentarian strongholds in the surrounding countryside. For long periods there was little action and there were several sallies forth from the castle, for example an attack on a Parliamentarian manor house at Thornton-in-Craven in July 1643 which resulted in loss of life.

The Parliamentarians drew up canon on the hills to the west and south of the castle and while there was some damage, the stout walls of the castle were strong enough to withstand the siege. The battle of Marston Moor, in which the Royalist troops under Prince Rupert were routed by Lord Fairfax and his men, marked the beginning of the end for the castle garrison. Several Royalists fled from the battle to seek refuge at Skipton, only to die there from their wounds.

The absence of Colonel Lambert from the siege at the battle (he was to become Governor of York afterwards) prompted several sorties by the besieged garrison and a number of soldiers were buried at Holy Trinity after their deaths in these skirmishes.

One particular sortie was to take part in an attempt to relieve Helmsley Castle, another besieged Royalist stronghold, but the attack was repelled. Another show of defiance came on February 17 1645 when Sir John Mallory, commander of the garrison, despatched 150 mounted troops to Keighley, where the Parliamentary commander, Colonel Brandling, was away. Riding through the snow they fell on the town early in the morning and the surprise attack claimed 100 prisoners, booty and livestock. However, weighed down with baggage, they were tardy on their return and Colonel Lambert, who was not far off, fell on them from behind. The prisoners turned on their captors and 20 Royalists were slain and 20 more taken prisoner. The remainder were pursued right back to the gates of the castle and Major Hughes, leader of the expedition, died of wounds almost immediately after reaching safety.

It was this assault which probably persuaded General Fairfax to conclude that the time had come to end Skipton's defiant resistance and in spring of 1645 the siege hardened. Skipton was the last Royalist castle in Yorkshire but with the gradual decline of the King's cause, it's fate was sealed. Bolton Castle had been defended by a garrison of Wensleydale militia who were reduced to earing horse flesh and, with continuing Royalist reverses and a harsh winter approaching, the Skipton garrison clearly foresaw that further resistance would mean loss of life and severe depredations. When Bolton Castle and Sandal were finally taken, further resistance was futile and negotiations began for the handover of the castle between Sir John Mallory, in charge of the garrison, and Colonel Richard Thornton, commander of the forces before the castle. The terms were generous. The castle was handed over to Parliament together with its ammunition, cannons and provisions but the honour of the garrison was intacat. Led by their governor, Sir John, the besieged marched out of the fortification with trumpets sounding, colours flying and drums beating. Prisoners held in the castle were released while the Royalists supporters were granted free passage to march to the side of King Charles I, to one of his garrisons or to return home. Sick or wounded members of the garrison stayed in Skipton until they had recovered, God willing, and were provided with good accommodation until they were fit to return home.

Skipton paid the price for its Royalist sympathies and Oliver Cromwell ordered the castle to be "slighted". This process involved demolishing or weakening the castle's defences so much that it would never more be able to withstand the advances of Parliament. The castle had been extensively damaged (although the eastern, inhabited portion was relatively untouched as this posed no military threat and the Parliamentarian generals in the north, Lambert and Fairfax, were friends of the Clifford family and unlikely to sanction unnecessary damage)

Lady Anne Clifford, after taking control of the castle, set about a rebuilding programme, restoring the castle as a place to live rather than a military outpost. For example, the flat, strong roof which had maintained canon was replaced by a sloping and slated roof, the walls were rebuilt with thinner versions and more glazed windows. A new entrance to the castle was built, facing south, with a steep flight of steps leading through the gateway.

Lady Anne Clifford was instrumental in restoring the castle and she has an almost iconic place in the town's annals. Her biography has been adequately detailed elsewhere but the essential details are as follows. She was born in the castle in 1590 and married in 1609 Richard Sackville, the earl of Dorset. Widowed in 1624, she then married Philip Herbert, the earl of Pembroke, a man described as "an ignoramus, a common swearer, a bully and a coward" and in another source as "a brutal simpleton". Upon the death of her father, the lands and rights passed into the hands of her uncle and she fought a long and at times bitter battle to enforce her rights. This was an age when women were not allowed to hold property but she won her case in the end, finally coming into possession of Skipton Castle and the other Clifford lands in the north when Henry Clifford died in 1643. This was of course midway through the Civil War and she had to see the castle slighted before restoration could begin.

In the 18th and 19th centuries the castle became increasingly dilapidated. Its owners, the Tufton family, were based in the south and by 1956, when the Fattorini family purchased the castle, it was in a bad state of repair. Happily the new owners have spent considerable sums in restoring the castle to its former glories and it now can justifiably claim to be one of the finest medieval castles in the north of England.

The Walk proceeds from the castle through a gateway into the church of Holy Trinity next door.

3: Holy Trinity

Enter the Holy Trinity churchyard through the gates. The church welcomes visitors (please be respectful) but allow additional time for the Walk if you plan to go inside.

THE first church at the top of what is now the High Street appeared shortly after the Norman Conquest. It is generally accepted that the same Robert de Romille who received the lordship of Skipton and set about building a castle also was instrumental in building a church to look after his soul. A wooden structure, probably without its imposing tower, no trace of this original building is left.

In around 1300 work was begun on the modern building, on the site of the modern tower thanks to grants from the monks at Bolton Priory. The church was considerably extended in the latter part of the 15th century when the choir was continued to its present extent. The interesting features inside the church are adequately dealt with elsewhere, not least in the church's own publications. The aim of this chapter is to deal with the effect of the church on the town, to which it forms such an elegant top.

The church was closely connected with the Clifford family – five earls of Cumberland, three countesses and four of their children are buried there.

During the civil war when Skipton was under siege, or more accurately intermittent blockade, the church suffered badly. Parliamentarian troops defaced the tombs of Henry, the first earl of Clifford and Francis Lord Clifford and the steeple suffered badly from canon ball hits. It was Lady Anne Clifford, who restored the castle, who set about ensuring that church too was rebuilt. On the north east pinnacle of the tower a tablet is inscribed pointing out her work.

Over the years the church has not been without its problems, not least being struck by lightning three times, in 1766, 1853 and 1925, and in January 1841 the church narrowly escaped being destroyed by fire but the outbreak was discovered quickly enough.

On June 19 1853 there was a severe thunderstorm and the church was struck by lightning, during a service and just as the psalm before the sermon was ended – which must at least have had great dramatic effect. Stones from the roof fell into the aisle and a stove pipe also crashed to the floor, spilling soot over the congregation who were terrified but uninjured. The Craven Herald, then only six issues old, recorded that a stone weighing about a ton had fallen from the tower and embedded itself in the flags below. Fortunately the vicar and a local surgeon called Birtwistle had not been in their pew at the time, records the Herald, or they would have suffered severe injury as large stones were found where they might have been sitting. Repairs cost £1,470 with the patronal Christ Church of Oxford donating £620.

There was one beneficial outcome to the episode. The opportunity was taken to lay nine to 12 inches of concrete on the floor – and for good reason. A report into the sanitary condition of burial vaults and graves in the church noted that: "every available space beneath the flooring of the parish church has been used for ages as a depository of the dead and it passes belief how large a quantity of putrefying matter has in this way been disposed of. Even now the vaults are in some cases gorged with corruption and all along the aisles and in the porch are graves filled with human remains. In most instances the only partition between the living and the dead is a single slab of stone and a few inches of earth. These offered but a very imperfect barrier to the escape of noxious effluvia and slowly therefore, but incessantly, the gaseous products of decomposition were effused into the atmosphere of the church. But at the night services, established in 1843 when gas was introduced into the church, when the air became rarefied by the warmth of stoves and burning gas the rank vapours were drawn out in uncontrollable profusion. It is impossible to say what mischief was done by this and how many, while worshipping within the sanctuary, have breathed the atmosphere of corruption and have sickened unto death".

It was not to be the last time that the church was struck by lightning. On

April 8 1925 the church was again hit and the organ was completely destroyed by fire.

Skipton's parish church registers are a mine of facts about the church and the town for those willing to plough through them. But what one wonders is one to make of the curious entry for December 19 1618: "John Jackson, a taylor, of Leedes, was wounded at Skipton and there dyed and was buried after the coroner had satt on hime"!

We often think of vandalism as a modern day phenomenon but in fact our predecessors were far from blameless. On November 1 1817 the pillars of the church gates were pushed over and demolished. The churchwardens offered the then huge sum of 20 guineas reward for information leading to a conviction but without any success

The first organist at Skipton seems to have been one Jonathan Jackson, appointed in 1809. The church evidently found it difficult to pay his successor, Charles Moraine and hit upon the novel idea of allowing him to charge a rent on the pews in the church's organ gallery. When the post became vacant later the church opened negotiations with a Miss Elizabeth Dodd, then living in the Liverpool Blind Asylum. She was taken on at a rate of £30 a year but a resolution was passed that "unless the organist can play better in three months" she would be given her notice. Miss Jackson evidently did improve for she was to retain the office for the next 37 years, dying at the age of 81 in 1891. She would have been there when the new organ, built by FW Jardine and Co of Manchester was installed at a cost of £700 in 1875. Its replacement, after the lightning strike of 1925, was constructed by Rushworth and Dreaper, of Liverpool, and cost £2,900.

A full list of the vicars of Skipton is kept within the church but a few are notable.

Thomas Sutton, installed as vicar in 1665 was singularly intolerant, particularly of Quakers, a movement which has a long and strong history in the town (as we shall see later). He made the following entry in the register: "Feb 5 1666, Jonathan, the son of John Stott, of Skipton, Quaker, christened by I knowe not whom and buried as they pleased at Bradley." John Stott certainly appears to have got right up the vicar's nose for in 1871 he demanded of him money for "sacramental wine, marrying him, baptising his children and churching his wife". Stott denied any liability, claiming that the priest had performed none of these services. But it was a fruitless task to take on officialdom and Rev Sutton obtained goods to the value of £1 16 shillings and 8 pence. Other Quakers were sent to York prison at his instigation for not attending church services.

A meeting was held on July 6 1771 to discuss the behaviour of the parish clerk, Joseph Crowther, who seemingly enjoyed his liquor. Several complaints were brought to the meeting about his conduct, the most serious being that Mr Crowther regularly turned up for parish duties well and truly sloshed as we might say today. Back in those days the churchwardens phrased it: "In several Sabbath days and times before then, the said Joseph Crowther, in time of divine service in the parish church was drunk, or very much intoxicated with liquor and behaved in a very indecent, irreverent and scandalous manner, to the great dishonour of God, the church and of all good people."

That was not all. Mr Crowther's duties also included running a school in Skipton, the clerk's school, "which is annexed to the clerkship". However, his devotion to the bottle meant that he had "shamefully neglected" these duties. The poor children of the parish were deprived of their lessons and remained illiterate.

The meeting resolved to sack Mr Crowther but, even in these pre-industrial tribunal days, there was a right of appeal granted "to prevent any imputation of ill usage or want of candour". Mr Crowther was given the opportunity to appear at a meeting in the vestry seven days later between the hours of four and six to show why he should not be sacked. Mr Crowther did in fact turn up, as the account book shows, but the churchwardens had their case ready. Churchwarden John Heelis proved that he had been drunk during service (how is not specified). Thomas Mitchell and Thomas Baker also proved (again no details of this proof) that he had neglected his teaching duties "in so shameful a manner that they and others, having large families, were totally deprived of the benefit of the said school and not being of ability to pay for the schooling and learning of their children, their children are by such neglect prevented of the means of acquiring a more comfortable livelihood and must remain illiterate."

George Lowcock also joined those who condemned Mr Crowther. He said that Crowther received the salary but did no good in the school. Further witnesses spoke of his drunkenness and the poor parish clerk appeared to be subdued by the weight of evidence. He could call upon no witnesses to dispute the charges.

His fate was put to the vote and, with 10 in favour, four against and nine abstaining, Crowther was sacked. A meeting four weeks later was called to appoint a successor but no candidate was forthcoming.

Within a year the parish account book noted that Crowther had died, on June 15 1772 and, curiously, it states that on his death the office became vacant. This time there was better luck at finding a successor. A further parish meeting was called, on July 6 1772, exactly a year after Crowther had been sacked, and Sylvester Heelis, presumably a relation of the John Heelis who had denounced him as a drunkard, was elected as the new parish clerk. Crowther may also take credit at least for providing new bells for the church, an incident related in the appendices

1771 was also the year in which a young Welshman called John Parry came to take up the post of vicar at Skipton but it seems he was at best odd, at worst downright insane. While he was to remain in his post until 1778, in 1776 the parish was forced to place the following advert in the Leeds Mercury: "A curate to do the constant duty of the parish church of Skipton is immediately required. Constant residence will be expected." In the same year the churchwardens' accounts record a payment of 12 shillings and 11 pence expenses for "seeking the vicar when lost" and in 1778 the parish register refers to "The Reverend John Parry Vicar (but insain)". His creditors achieved a court order taking sums from the benefice to meet his debts, once the costs of providing a proper person to carry out the religious duties had been deducted. For the next 65 years the Parish Church was without a resident incumbent, the vicar at Kildwick taking on the duties with a curate at Skipton

Thomas Marsden, vicar from 1790 to 1806 was a popular priest. It was related that he would travel to Embsay at feast time to sort out church taxes with the locals and while there would enter into the sporting competitions. No-one could beat him at quoits and throwing the bar and he even seems to have been pretty handy at wrestling matches, there being one stout countryman however, who would throw him in the ring every time. However Marsden was involved in a bitter power struggle with the headmaster of Ermysted's Grammar School which is covered in the chapter on that institution.

A clock has existed on the tower since before 1769, when a bill to pay for repairs is documented. In 1826 a meeting of parishioners resolved that the clock was so old and out of repair that a new one should be purchased, although at a cost of less than £100. It was not until 1835 that the clock appeared however, made by Titus Bancroft of Sowerby Bridge and having two dials, on the south side of the tower looking down the High Street and one looking west. In 1899 the current clock was installed at a cost to the town of £285 and built by Messers Potts of Leeds. It is still going strong 100 years later. Incidentally, it is a bone of contention among a good few Skiptonians, that the trees planted in front of the church have in fact obscured the view of the building, not least the view of the clock and they are deprived of the chance of telling the time from the High Street. Others would be outraged if they were cut down.

In 1916 Holy Trinity almost became a cathedral. Before that time the area was part of the diocese of Ripon but as that ancient town had remained a small, perhaps isolated, market town, the centre of population had shifted to towns like Keighley and Bradford. It was proposed to split the diocese in two, roughly north to south, creating a new see of the Craven archdeaconry and Bradford. Skipton was roughly the central point of the proposed new diocese and its ancient parish church would have made a fitting cathedral. However that was the minority view. There was a stronger lobby for Bradford to be the base for the diocese given the experience of the difficulties involved in having bishop and cathedral in a country market town in the north and its main centre of population a large city at the opposite end of the diocese. Another consideration was the fact that Holy Trinity was tightly enclosed with little, if any possibility of expansion. The same could not be said of St Peter's, in Bradford, and so the opportunity was lost. Even so, the archdeaconry of Craven has always asserted a degree of independence since the formation of the Bradford Diocese was confirmed by King George V's Order in Council of 1919. The official history of the Bradford diocese described Craven as "run almost like a see within a see".

Before leaving, it is interesting to note Dawson's 1882 comments on funerals in the town. He laments: "With regret it must be said that our Craven funeral ceremonies are fast losing their beauty and simplicity... Than the rural burial in Craven of 60 or 80 years ago no sight could be more touching, none more pleasing. There were not then the trumpery gee-gaws which are, alas! deemed so indispensable nowadays but which seem to throw around the solemn rite an air rather of hollow mockery and irreverence than of sorrow and sanctity." The local custom so lamented by Dawson appears to be a profusion of children and young women, dressed in white and holding white ribbons attached to the coffin. The funeral itself was "bright with hymns and chants" and flowers were in abundance. Until about 1800 torchlight funerals were also popular and a woman who had died at the birth of her first child was traditionally buried at midnight. Generally her coffin was carried under a white sheet, the corners of which were supported by four females.

However, the practice of night burials was not welcomed by Rev Robert Dyneley, a curate at Holy Trinity. A town meeting resolved that "upon the representation of Rev Robert Dyneley that great inconvenience does frequently arise from the custom of delaying funerals till a very late and unreasonable hour in the evening" in order to prevent such delay "which in most cases is alike inconvenient to the officiating minister and the well disposed part of the parishioners, it is ordered that all funerals be henceforth solemnised at or before six o'clock in summer and at or before four o'clock in the winter."

The Walk leaves Holy Trinity by a narrow gateway to the right down a short flight of steep narrow steps towards Mill Bridge. Children should be carefully supervised as the steps disgorge onto a narrow pavement beside a busy road. Proceed along the main road and over the canal bridge.

4: Mill Bridge

THE area adjoining Holy Trinity is probably the oldest settled part of the town and dates back to Saxon times, predating the castle. Our route takes us past the Castle pub, built around 1800. Next door is the impressive facade of Varley's solicitors' premises, Mill Bridge House, built about 150 years ago. It is one of the few houses in Skipton faced with limestone. In the early 1900s it was a private school and rooms at the back served as the practice rooms for Skipton Band for many years. The third of the impressive buildings on this short stretch is the property of David Hill, estate agent and land valuer. This building dates from about 1780 and for many years was a public house, the New Ship Inn. In 1805 there began its long association with the Alderson family which lasted until 1917. Older Skiptonians have memories of a fox kept in a cage outside the pub and this was the home of the Craven Hunt for many years. In 1974 time was finally called on the pub.

Across the road is Amy Egan's shop which at one time housed Skipton's horse drawn fire engines. The original black doors can be seen on either side of the entrance to the shop. In those days the fire service only turned out to those buildings whose owners took out insurance. Houses covered had metal fire insurance tokens pinned to them and several of these survive in the Craven museum. If the property had no metal plate signifying it was covered, well then tough luck! Some claim that the artist's cottage adjacent is the oldest property in Skipton.

We are now at Mill Bridge, a double bridge crossing both Eller Beck and the canal.

The old ford, over the beck was replaced by a bridge in 1628 (the canal was to follow more than a century later) and the charge was made to the wapentakes (administrative districts) of Staincliffe and Ewecross. Mill Bridge now takes us over both the canal and Eller Beck, a tributary of the river Aire. The road leading up the hill is Raikes Road, Raikes being a Norse word for steep hill, and was the original road from Skipton, part of the Keighley to Kendal turnpike, to Gargrave and beyond. At the foot of The Royal Oak pub can still be seen the old cobbled road. A row of houses adjoining the pub, below today's Raikes road, uses this old cobbled road as access. The Royal Oak (whose name reflects the town's royalist loyalties) was built by 1815 although an earlier pub stood on the site. The yard behind the pub was used for the stabling of horses in connection with the castle and the boskins, the vertical partitions which separate horses in a stable, for 32 horses are still visible in the two stables in the yard. Also still visible are the hay loft doors (with circular window above) and inside the cottages are internal doorways which connected these dwellings (presumed to be those of ostlers) to the stables. The stables were for many years occupied by a well known local firm, Lawson's, cabinet makers, joiners, undertakers and upholsterers. The Royal Oak must have the lowest storey in Skipton as there are two storeys below the present ground floor at about the level of Eller Beck and below the canal.

Today Eller Beck goes underneath the bridge, alongside this extension of the canal. The canal is not the main Leeds to Liverpool waterway but a branch heading north from Skipton Canal Basin and extending just 300 yards. Called the Springs Canal, it was built to enable limestone quarried at Haw Bank, between Skipton and Embsay, to be transported via the waterways more economically. Stone from the quarry was transported in horse drawn rail buckets along a route which originally terminated high above the canal by the castle. The stone was simply dropped down chutes into the waiting barges. It must have been a hazardous venture and eventually a new route was cut, bringing the stone wagons to a terminus much closer to the water's edge. A separate walk along the towpath into Skipton Woods leads past the end of this rail line and one of the metal chutes can still be seen, rusting and overgrown, extending out over the canal.

After crossing the bridge continue along the road before turning to the right into Chapel Hill

Arial: The High Street and Springs Canal

Above:
The broad High Street and popular market

Left:
Sir Mathew Wilson Bt

It was good enough for Richard III – The Black Horse

Telephone box sentries outside the privately built Town Hall

Skipton Castle - Henceforth

Conduit Court "...It was mine own house, which I thought my castle"

The Chapel of St John the Evangelist, a Cromwellian stable

Holy Trinity, not enough space to be made a Cathedral

Pies, ale and Primrose Hill

Pine, fine wine and Chapel Hill

Springs Canal in early summer

Replica of Sewer Lamp, and wooden gutters on a canal side cottage

Left:
St Stephens overlooks the town

Below:
The view from Castle View Terrace, look high for the Roman Road

Three notable buildings stand at the foot of Chapel Hill at the junction with the main road. Pottery and Pine was originally known as West House and was originally a residential house. It was converted into retail use as the Sheepskin Warehouse in 1978 and was purchased by Pottery and Pine in 1986.

On the corner is Bob Wright's wine shop, the Wright Wine Company. This building was a working smithy right up to the mid 1970s when Jack Ward was the proprietor. It then became a wine shop and has been operated by Mr Wright since 1981. The building housed a fire engine in direct competition to the one run from just a few yards away and mentioned above. The roadway alongside Napier's restaurant, originally a farmhouse dating from about 1700, and the main road probably contains some of the oldest flagging in Skipton

Just beyond the Wright Wine Shop, up Raikes Road, is the old Skipton Pinfold where stray sheep were impounded by the Pinder. They were released upon payment of a fine and Skipton Police used to display a document listing the fines and who had paid them. Another pinfold was situated in Skipton by Pinder Bridge on Keighley Road. Behind the Old Pinfold was a tithe barn for the castle with a date stone of 1670. Our walk does not take us up this pleasant, leafy part of Skipton but a little further up the Raikes Road is the old cemetery behind high walls but still accessible. A little forlorn, or overgrown, it is considered by many to be a peaceful haven.

On the right on Chapel Hill is High Corn Mill, occupied today by Ledgard and Wynn furnishers where a corn mill was recorded in 1310. Until the 19th century malt money, or a toll had to be paid to those using the mill. The Earl of Thanet, owner of Skipton Castle, took great care to protect his rights as evidenced by a court case heard at York in 1762 in which the earl and the tenant of the mill attempted to assert their ancient rights to what was in effect a cartel which ensured that all corn bought or traded in Skipton had to be ground at the mill. Not only could Skiptonians not have their corn ground elsewhere but the earl, as lord of the manor, had the right to take a 24th part of all corn ground at his mill as his own. The earl, records Dawson, had 50 witnesses who testified that the earl of Thanet had threatened action against people who attempted to build their own mills to bypass those rights. One Esther Chippindale, who had lived in Skipton for 50 years, deposed that her father had kept an inn in Skipton. About 35 or 40 years previously he had set up a steel mill for grinding his own malt but Thomas, then earl of Thanet had "sent to him to pull it down and carry his corn to the mill, which he accordingly did and from that time he carried all his malt and corn to be ground at the mill". The defendants, William Lonsdale and Richard Birtwhistle, whom Dawson describes as being representatives of a large body of objectors, disputed the custom which the earl and his mill tenant sought to establish as greatly detrimental to the poor inhabitants and argued that "foreign" – ie from outside the town – mill owners used frequently to come into the town to trade in "foreign" corn. Interestingly they quoted the case of one Benjamin Smith who had built his own mill and sold it door to door. When the mill owner heard of this rather than beginning a law suit he subtly resorted to blackmail. The Earl of Thanet's bailiff just happened to be Benjamin Smith's nephew, and he was informed that "he should not continue to be employed as bailiff any longer unless he could influence his uncle so far as to cause him to desist from using the steel mill and thereupon the said Benjamin Smith gave over the practice rather than expose his kinsman to the hazard of losing so beneficial a place."

The Earl of Thanet was successful in his litigation and the custom of paying "soke" money was upheld. It was known in the town as "mant money" – mant being a corruption of malt. By the mid 19th century the custom was still technically in place but was observed only on a very small scale. The story is that the last miller to receive it, one Thomas King, approached the Earl of Thanet seeking a reduction in his rent for the mill and was reminded of the mant money. King replied, truthfully in all probability, that it was worth next to nothing whereupon the Earl replied that if that was the case he would scrap it – and did so. Whether Mr King earned his reduction is not known.

In 1954 the castle estate sold the mill and it was acquired by George Leatt who restored and repaired the mill, opening it to the public as a folk museum. Its chief attraction was a working mill wheel, one of which, together with gearing mill stones, came from Markington near Ripon. After the death of Mr Leatt in 1985 the property was sold and a number of firms, including Ledgard and Wynn now occupy the mill.

It is worth recording that the mill probably now employs more people than at any time in its life. Inside there has been a sympathetic restoration and computer based, high technology industries now find the old mill a home.

Further up Chapel Hill is the Wesleyan Chapel, built in 1791 and rebuilt in 1821. This was to be replaced by a newer, even larger chapel on Water Street in 1865 and this building then became home to a Wesleyan School. The school was to follow the chapel to Water Street in 1891. At the time of writing there are plans to turn this grand building into flats.

On the wall by the Vogue clothes shop is a plaque marking the spot where John Wesley preached to the town. He had originally ridden to Skipton to preach in the Market Place but as it was raining (!) instead he preached from outside the home of John Garforth at the foot of Raikes Road. It was not John Wesley's sole link with Skipton. In 1747 he had applied for the post of headmaster of Ermysted's Grammar School while still at Oxford but was turned down (the incident is fully recounted in the chapter on Ermysted's School).

The walk now returns back to Mill Bridge This is the only part of the walk where steps have to be redoubled. Take the path on the left down to the grassed area and the towpath, straight ahead leads into Skipton Woods. A diversion up here lasts about 40 minutes and leads through tranquil scenery. About 25 yards ahead, on the left hand side, can be seen the old waterwheel.

Unfortunately wheelchair access to the towpath here is not possible. It is advised to proceed down Water Street and rejoin the walk by St Stephen's School. Access to Springs Canal is possible via the pocket park on Canal Street. Access to the Prazza at the junction of Springs Canal and the Leeds-Liverpool is available from the Coach Street car park. Toilets for disabled people are close by.

The walk has brought us to a pleasant part of the town which was cleaned up by the Civic Society, which successfully argued that this would make a pleasant approach to the canal path behind the castle and into Skipton Woods – previously one had to scramble down extremely narrow steps next to Stanforths.

On one side is the Springs Canal and on the other Eller Beck flows under the Old Mill. The old ford crossed here. If Eller Beck is low you can carefully look under the bridge and see two phases of bridge building. Looking at the key stone in the centre top you can see which side was the extension. Eller Beck re-emerges having run under the roadway for about 25 metres. On this spot, now a peaceful haven, two cottages used to stand. They were so low down that effluent from the sinks and water closets could not be drained into the sewers to they were condemned and pulled down.

Take the route under the canal bridge and continue along the towpath to the canal basin.

A strange brick building overhangs the canal on the left hand side. Its purpose has never been satisfactorily explained as it clearly is a hastily erected addition to the original. The building served as a fish and chip shop but the overhang cannot have aided queuing. The most likely explanation, if the most unromantic one, is that it was a toilet for the house, the waste dropping straight into the canal! This is one of the most ancient buildings in Skipton and a certain candidate for the most neglected.

5: Water Street and canal

The walk is now taking us back along the Springs Canal to the junction with the main Leeds-Liverpool Canal at Canal Basin, where in 1998 an area was opened to provide a picnic area.

TO the right of the towpath is Back Water Street. Back in the 1930s these houses were crowded premises with no running water. After World War Two they were earmarked for demolition and a new road system was planned for this area, which lies just to the west of the High Street. After years of deliberation, it never came off and these pleasant houses survived to become desirable properties. Beyond them is Water Street, which becomes Gargrave Road and the main route to Lancashire and the west, but it is a relatively recent addition to the road network. Back in 1824 the Trustees of the Keighley to Kendal toll road were anxious to make a better road to avoid the steep and narrow Raikes Road leading north westwards out of Skipton. When the new Gargrave Road was conceived it was hoped that it would continue straight across Springs Canal and Eller Beck to link up to the High Street and then across towards Otley Road and out to the east. That never came about because of a lack of money (a familiar tale in Skipton's road network) and instead, when the new Gargrave Road section of the Keighley to Kendal Toll Road was built in the 1830s it joined the old Water Street. The new road "looked longingly across the canal, the brook and the mill goyt into the promised land of the High

Street".

Water Street has several interesting buildings. An imposing Wesleyan Methodist Chapel was built in the mid 1860s (its foundation stone was laid on February 9 1864). The chapel was closed following its merger with the Gargrave Road Methodist Chapel. This building is now owned by North Yorkshire County Council and contains the offices of the local education department. It also contains the offices of the Registrar of Births, Marriages and Deaths. Confetti blowing around the steps and impressive columns indicates that another Skipton couple has been "spliced" there!

Also in Water Street is the school. Opened as a Wesleyan Methodist School in 1890, in 1955 it was bought by West Riding County Council, modernised and opened as Water Street County Primary School. Further along Water Street is a former school, opened by mill owner Christopher Sidgwick in 1840 to educate the children of workers employed at his mills in the town. It lasted for just four years when the pupils moved to Christ Church School and the building has undergone a number of commercial uses. Today it is a restaurant serving Mexican food.

Back to the walk, which proceeds to the Coach Street bridge. New houses on the right were built in 1995 on the site of the Mill Goyt, or dam, which provided power for a factory which existed here as early as 1311. By the early 18th century it was used for glazing paper and was then sold to John Hallam for worsted spinning and weaving. It became part of the Dewhurst empire in 1872 as a workshop for making spindles and the goyt became known as Spindle Mill Dam. The flow of water was controlled by sluice gates, whose remnants can still be seen on the beck side just after Mill Bridge. On the left, on the opposite side of the canal are iron street lamps, modern replicas of original methane gas lamps, powered by methane gas from the sewers

Around here was sited a ducking stool used for the punishment of women. It was situated by a pool, although it is unclear whether this was a part of the rather shallow Eller Beck or a separate pool - possibly one which was to become the mill dam. The first reference to the ducking stool came in 1734 when a payment was made to a William Bell for the chair but it is likely it was in place before this date. There are other references to payments for repairs to the ducking stool in 1743 and 1768 and the practice appears to have been dispensed with around 1770.

The walk continues under Coach Street bridge to the new piazza at Canal Basin, where the Leeds-Liverpool Canal meets the Springs Branch extension.

Skiptonians today look upon the canal which flows through the town as a pleasant amenity, one which greatly enhances the environmental aspect of the town. Pleasure boats form a welcome contrast to the impositions of the motor vehicle which intrude on so many towns. But the canal is far more than a draw for tourists and pleasant walkway for locals. It is, along with the market, the whole raison d'etre for Skipton's development. Without it the modern town may well have been much smaller.

The Leeds-Liverpool Canal, one of the country's greatest waterways, reached Skipton in April 1773. It might have been a lot earlier. In 1744 a Bill was laid before Parliament to make the river Aire navigable from Cottingley to Inghay Bridge, just outside Skipton, the aim being to secure cheaper limestone but it was Lord Thanet, owner of the Castle, who blocked the move. A letter from the time states: "We suppose Lord Thanet's opposition proceeds either from party or pique that he is not at the head of the affair, nor has been sufficiently consulted or perhaps he may imagine that as his estates are mostly grass farms and as the cloth makers send up great numbers of horses and cattle to agist (graze) upon and near his Lordships estates and as the navigation may make grass and hay more plentiful in the places from whence those cattle are sent". In other words, he was attempting to protect a private monopoly.

Despite the Earl's initial opposition, this was the canal age and the demand for cheaper transport, in particular for coal, was huge. Committees were formed and the route, or rather routes, were surveyed. In 1769 an important meeting was held in Bradford and, although it did not touch the city, the canal's estimated value to the town there was so great that most of the early meetings to discuss the project were held there. Bradford men held many of the chief offices in the early days and for many years the affairs of the canal company were conducted from a head office in that city. Eventually a route was agreed upon, the Yorkshire shareholders of the Leeds-Liverpool Canal company being in the majority and it was decided to obtain Parliamentary powers to proceed with the construction of the canal. Interestingly the initial route sought included a branch line to Settle, although that was eventually dropped due to disagreements among landowners along the route.

At a meeting held in Skipton it was decided to ask Richard Wilson of

Leeds, Mathew Wilson of Eshton Hall, John Clayton of Carr Hall, Colne, and Mr Hustler of London to attend in London to press the case for a bill to Parliament allowing for the construction of a canal.

In May 1770 the Bill had passed both Houses and the capital authorised was £260,000 in £100 shares. The first general assembly of shareholders was held in the Black Horse, Skipton, on June 20 1770 and the attendance was so great that the meeting had to adjourn to Skipton Castle where the first committee of management was appointed. Among the names of the 23 appointed were Peter Garforth of Skipton, William Chippendale, a mercer, of Skipton and John Clayton, of Carr Hall. Shares worth £185,000 were taken up and that rose to above £200,000 after a second meeting at Burnley

The canal was begun in three sections; Douglas to Liverpool, Skipton to Bingley and Shipley to Leeds but the purchase of land and settlement of landowners' claims was a long and tedious business. There does not appear to have been much difficulty in obtaining land in Yorkshire and in many cases the landowners had purchased shares so it was in their interests for the project to proceed. A favourite meeting place was the White Bear at Cross Hills and Peter Garforth was heavily involved in persuading landowners to sell their land to the canal company.

The actual work of cutting the canal on the Skipton section started in 1771 and proceeded at a good pace. Much of the canal was designed by the famous canal engineer James Brindley, who had a taste for extravagant designs, such as the aqueduct over the road at Kildwick. However, these were more expensive than swing bridges or diversions, and the expense soon put paid to such feats of civil engineering. The Skipton section was opened on April 7 1773. The Leeds Intelligencer reported: "That part of the grand canal from Bingley to Skipton was opened and two boats laden with coal arrived at the last-mentioned place which were sold at half the price they had hitherto given for that most necessary convenience of life, which is a recent instance, among others, of the great use of canals in general. On which occasion the bells were set a-ringing at Skipton, there were also bonfires, illuminations and other demonstrations of joy."

The company appointed a toll gatherer in Skipton on April 15 of that year at a weekly wage of 18 shillings. Work progressed and in 1774 the canal was driven from Skipton to Holme Bridge in Gargrave. The York Courant reported that "a boat laden with coals went so high on the canal, making betwixt Leeds and Liverpool, as Holme Bridge above Skipton, on which account the bells of Gargrave were set a-ringing and other demonstrations of joy."

Unfortunately, Holme Bridge was the headwater of the canal for some years to come as the company ran out of capital and concentrated on consolidating the sections which were opened. It was not until 1816 that the complete waterway between Leeds and Liverpool were opened, and that only after long controversy and litigation.

Meanwhile at Skipton the agents of Lord Thanet, son of the man who had opposed the river Aire navigation, decided that a canal branch to their master's quarries should be constructed. The canal company had refused to alter their line to allow improved access to his quarries and the result was the Springs Branch, a mere quarter mile in length, which led off from Skipton Basin to behind the castle, where limestone was quarried. The Act was passed in 1773 and the Springs Canal was driven soon afterwards. It certainly helped the Thanet coffers and limekilns were constructed alongside the canal to profit from the easier access to lime. A major customer was the Bradford Limekiln Company, which purchased 62,815 tons between 1781 and 1783.

In 1785 the Leeds-Liverpool Canal Company took over the lease of the quarries and opened a new quarry at Haw Bank, near Embsay. By 1794 the Springs Branch had been extended by 240 yards and a tramway had been built from Haw Bank to ease transportation of the stone. Originally the tramway ended high above the head of the canal extension and was dropped about 100 feet into the boats by long chutes. Not only did this damage the boats, but it was also noisy and Lord Thanet asked for the tramroad to be extended to the main canal. He was turned down, although in 1836 the tramroad was diverted near its canal terminus bringing the wagons to the canal side at a much lower height. The stone could then be dropped in from a height of about 20 feet, with much less damage to the boats and grief to the ears of the castle owners.

Mike Clarke, in his book the Leeds and Liverpool Canal, tells of particularly good business during the American Civil War, quoting 31 canal boats at a time, each loading 500 tons a day, waiting in the canal for limestone from Haw Bank.

Much of the early traffic on the waterway was coal. It could be transported into the non-mining areas in much greater bulk and therefore at a much cheaper price. This enabled the mills of Skipton to thrive (all were built on the canalside). However, there were few mills in Skipton at the time of the canal construction and the fact that it diverted north to the town rather than headed in a more direct route due west was initially due to the need to take produce from the area out rather than bring goods in. The chief product was limestone which was extracted from the numerous quarries in the area while lead ore from the prosperous Grassington mines were brought by pony train via Hetton to Gargrave to be loaded on the boats at Holme Bridge.

The driving of the canal through Skipton must have meant the removal of a certain amount of property. Winterwell Hall, a house of some size occupied by the Lambert family, whose most famous son was the Parliamentarian Civil War general John Lambert.

Opposite the canal basin can be seen an old building, with the word Duckett's clearly visible. Duckett's was a prolific house building business established in the second half of the 19th century and flourishing well into the 20th century but this building has been empty for many years, its future the subject of considerable speculation.

With one's back to the canal junction, the walk heads off across the car park to the left, round past the Millfield buildings, standing between two car parks.

The oldest of the buildings which form an island in the midst of the car park is the Primitive Methodist Chapel, which was built in 1835 and closed as a place of worship in 1880 when a larger building was put up on Gargrave Road. A bicycle shop existed here before the war but between 1945 and 1974 its use changed once more, to Skipton Fire Station. An interesting account of the early days of the fire brigade can be found in the Craven Household Almanack of 1905. Run by the Urban District Council, in the case of a fire, residents were advised that: "the alarm should be set on from the fire alarm box on the wall at the Ship Corner by breaking the glass and pulling the knob. The person giving the alarm must then proceed immediately to the fire station in the Dockyard, Coach Street, to give information as to locality of fire. The first to give such alarm will receive one shilling from the superintendent." The brigade could be contacted by telephone, number 19, but as there were so few people with phones at the time, this advice may have been relatively useless (number 1 belonged to Lionel Dewhurst of Prospect Villa, 2 was Algernon Dewhurst of Aireville, while the Duke of Devonshire was listed at Bolton Abbey as 67). The cycle shop was owned by Bishop and Schroot and it is worth recording that here George Bishop and an engineer, Elijah Wroe, built Skipton's first car in 1897. This was probably not the same vehicle which Walter Morrison drove down the High Street in the same year but a separate, home-built affair.

The old chapel is now occupied by Craven College, who run it as a beauty salon, training students. The Coffee House was built as Parish Church Infants School, and for a time were the auction rooms.

Cross the bridge over Eller Beck to the left of Coffee House and then bear to the right, heading for steps at the top centre of the car park.

The car park in front of the old fire station stands on the site of Lower Commercial Street which ran directly north up the hill, forming a cross roads with Gargrave Road and Commercial Street which ran up the steep hill. The demolition era of the 1960s removed both Commercial Streets and for a time there was mooted a ring road through the town. Happily, this never came to pass and Commercial Street was redeveloped for housing, called Street Stephen's Close, although access by road with Gargrave Road was reinstated by footpath only,

To the left is the Fisher Medical Centre. This modern, purpose-built premises for one of the two groups of medical practitioners in the town was opened on March 4 1995 by Dr Brian Fisher, whose father Annesley and grandfather George had been doctors in the town.

As a general rule, until the start of the National Health Service in 1948, the vast majority of general practitioners were single-handed operations, often based in their own homes. Skipton was no exception. As stated earlier, at least two of these doctors were based in the High Street. One, Dr Moran, was based in David Goldie's at the top of the High Street, while on the opposite side of the road at 2 High Street was Dr Bob Fisher from about 1895 until his death in 1937. He was the nephew of George Fisher, who was practicing from about 1890 until his death in 1939 from Swadford Street. His son, Annesley, practiced in Skipton from 1919 to 1954, originally in a surgery which was a wooden extension in the garden of 2 High Street, where his cousin, Bob, was also practicing.

In 1939 Annesley Fisher and Guy Ollerenshaw teamed up to form Britain's first group practice operating out of Hawthorn Cottages on Otley Street where they were to stay for many years until the practice outgrew its base, prompting the move to its current site.

Climb the steps or use the ramp at the top of the car park on to Gargrave Road and turn left. This new access has proved a great benefit for locals as well as those on the Millennium Walk.

On the right is Street Stephen's School and, at the top of the hill, St Stephen's Roman Catholic Church. The Catholic population of this country was subjected to discrimination, even persecution and it was not until 1842 that the church was built. Before that date Skipton's Catholics would gather on Belmont Bridge and then walk some five miles to Broughton Hall and the private chapel where missionary priests ministered to the needs of the community. The Tempest family have owned Broughton Hall and its estate from Norman times but refused to adopt the Protestant faith after the Reformation, at times to their discomfiture. Catholic masses were also said occasionally above Myers' shop in Albert Street, Skipton and in the Black Horse when owned by a Catholic family at the start of the 19th century.

A more permanent building to serve the Catholic community was started in 1835, when the site was purchased from William Chamberlain and Henry Ovington and the foundation stone was laid by Sir Charles Tempest on October 27 1836. The firm of Shuttleworth and Spink, who had just completed the Anglican Christ Church in the town, was engaged for the building work. However, the church was the subject of an acrimonious dispute between the Tempests and Fr Michael Trappes, who arrived as their chaplain in 1828 and appears to have been the driving force behind the building of the new church. On December 26 1836 he gave a supper for the workmen in the Cock and Bottle in Skipton to mark the completion of the roof (using oak from Broughton Hall estate). Sir Charles was unaware and took exception to what he considered an assumption of his authority. That sparked a row between the wealthy landowner and his private chaplain which ended with Father Trappes saying he would leave within a week and never set foot in Broughton Hall again.

Charles Tempest took control of the completion of the church but it was not to open for another five years, due to the dispute between the family and the diocese over authority of the new church, particularly with regard to choosing the incumbent priest. The bitterness between Tempest and Fr Trappes hindered matters. Tempest claimed that the priest owed him £120, a sum he had not accounted for in the building work, and Trappes refused to provide details which led to Tempest impounding the priest's remaining belongings, refusing to send them on to his new address. Tempest claimed that the building belonged to him as sole trustee, Trappes countering by affirming that the landowner had taken no interest in the building and had never mentioned any rights. Indeed, in one letter, he wrote: "I wish this matter was settled, it annoys me much and throughout the whole affair I consider that I have been shamefully treated and Tempest has had opportunity plenty to glut his thirst for revenge".

The dispute clearly could not continue – one wonders what the town's Catholics made of a finished church standing empty because of an unseemly row between the chief benefactor and the Church authorities. It ended when the Archbishop of Leeds, Dr John Briggs, agreed to Sir Charles having the right of nominating the priest and to the church being blessed and used for mass on condition that Sir Charles signed a paper stating that no call could be made upon the diocese for money towards maintenance of the priest or support of the mission. This agreement enabled the church to be opened by a High Mass conducted by Fr Thomas Peter Tempest (brother of Sir Charles) on September 15 1842. The church was named St Stephen's; it is believed because of the persuasion of Skipton merchant Baldisarro Porri, in honour of the church in his home town of Appiano, Italy. The first baptism, of Monica Jemima Porri, followed four days later and the church was solemnised for marriage in 1860 (the first being that of John Drysdale and Frances Jane Swire, of Embsay, on January 26 of that year). Fr Tempest was the first priest (it seems at the request of the parishioners and to the reluctance of Sir Charles) and his residence was above Porri's shop on Swadford Street but he was to leave in less than two years. The church was to be enlarged in 1853 as the Catholic community expanded through conversion and the arrival of Irish immigrants.

In 1914 Major Arthur Tempest, who had inherited the Tempest estates after the death of his brother, Sir Charles, in 1865, relinquished the Tempest's control over the parish, handing it to the diocese (Major Arthur was a real character – he was placed four times in the Grand National at Aintree). In 1991, with help from a grant from Skipton Town Council, the church was floodlit each night, a practice which continues today.

Like other religious communities in the town, the Catholics were keen to have their children instructed in the faith and a day school was established in 1849 above a shop in Albert Street. A proper building was desired and the school opened in 1854. It is interesting to note that Sir Charles abandoned his original intention to build the school halfway up the long drive to the church when his hopes of buying Holywell Cottage as a residence for the Catholic priest were thwarted by a nonconformist minister, Mr Sills, who would not move. Sir Charles, clearly a man to get his own way, accordingly built the school right next to the cottage. The Jesuits later bought the cottage and sold it to the diocese in 1914 for £450 and it became absorbed into the school. Interestingly, as this book is published, plans have been drawn up to build a new school halfway up the drive, where Sir Charles originally envisaged it. The school has proved extremely popular and has outgrown its premises, despite the addition of an infant block on the other side of the driveway, in 1895. These new plans are for a stepped building with the unusual concept of grass roofs.

Before moving on it is worth mentioning the establishment of a convent next to the church (on the right hand side as one looks up the drive) which now serves as the parish priest's residence. This was opened in 1861 and named St Monica's in remembrance of Monica Tempest, who had funded its foundation but died a year before it was completed. The convent was expanded and opened a boarding and day school for girls from five up to 18 (one notable ex-old girl was Elizabeth Peacock, Conservative MP for Batley and Spen through the 1980s until 1997 while Iain MacLeod also went there). Street Monica's flourished after the war for a time but then economic troubles set in and it finally closed in 1969.

Almost opposite the school are the new, and dare one say out of character, block of flats built in the 1970s on the site of the Primitive Methodist Chapel, built in 1878 and a rather imposing, Gothic building. It was demolished in the 1970s because the congregation could not pay for the upkeep of such a large building. Methodist worship was concentrated on St Andrew's Church on Newmarket Street.

The houses on the left were build on land originally owned by Ermysted's Grammar School in the early 1900s. Interestingly the deeds of at least one of the houses prohibits the staging of a number of events, including riotous parties or boxing matches without the express permission of the headmaster!

Opposite is Ermysted's Grammar School.

6: Ermysted's

ERMYSTED'S Grammar School for boys is renowned for its academic excellence. Somehow it survived the purge of selective schools in the second half of the 20th century and there has been little agitation within the town for it to turn "comprehensive". Its proud record in public examinations leads to frantic scenes of private tuition in the locality (and beyond) as anxious parents seek to ensure that their son passes through its doors. The high price of housing in and around Skipton is partly attributed to the desirability of sending children to the town's two grammar schools (the other being the Girls' High). Given Ermysted's respected and eminent position within the social make-up of the town, it is sometimes hard to believe that its history has at times been turbulent and, indeed, highly scandalous. Impeccably run now for many years, it was not always the case.

The first mention of the school is back in 1492, the year in which Christopher Columbus so famously discovered America. But the school goes back beyond this for 1492 was the year of Peter Toller's death, and his will mentions a bequest to the school. In 1548 a survey was made of church lands and Toller's gift of land came under its scope. The report noted that 120 boys were under instruction at the school under Stephen Ellis, "a good grammarian".

Toller's input was only discovered by the researches of a master at the school AM Gibbon, who was preparing a book to mark the school's 400th anniversary in 1948. Before that the school dated its start to Canon William

Ermsyted, who appears to have been from Craven but was a canon of St Paul's and a clerk of the King's Chancery. He witnessed at first hand the seizures of ecclesiastical lands by Henry VIII and Edward VI, including those given by Toller. He drew up an endowment deed for the continuance and development of the threatened school dated September 1 1548 leaving monies for the maintenance and upkeep of the school and giving clear instructions for the curriculum to be taught. In view of the fact that the same 120 or so boys were the first to be enrolled, under the same master, Stephen Ellis, the school considers that it is has an unbroken history gong back to the original founding of Peter Toller's school.

We have no details of where the school was originally located but Ermysted's newly-endowed school was situated at the bottom of Shortbank Road (a site which our walk will later cover) in a building which had originally been the chapel of the Knights Hospitallers of St John of Jerusalem. At the time of the Reformation it had fallen into the hands of Lord Henry Clifford, the Earl of Cumberland, Skipton Castle's owner, and was purchased from them by Ermysted. His deed of foundation laid down the rules for the school. Hours were from 6am to 6pm each day with a two hour interval in the summer and from 7am to 5 or 6pm in the winter. Every day certain psalms had to be sung and prayers said or the master became liable to a fine of 20 pence and, ultimately, dismissal. The vicar and churchwardens of Holy Trinity were his judge and jury with powers of dismissal for inappropriate conduct such as missing church. The same vicar and churchwardens also had the duty of appointing a new headmaster and, if they failed to do so within one month, that duty transferred to the rector and fellows of Lincoln College, Oxford (and should they too fail to elect someone then the right of appointment rested with the Dean and Chapter of St Paul's Cathedral). This duty was to have a significant repercussion in the history of the school.

That first headmaster in the new school, Stephen Ellis, had lost the income from church lands and he visited London in 1560 to the court of the exchequer to persuade the authorities to restore the income from Toller's bequest, a mission which proved successful, thus adding to the £9 15 shillings and 4 pence annual income from Ermysted's endowment the sum of £4, 4 shillings and 10 pence from Toller's bequest, a total of £14 per annum. That was a tidy sum for those times but poor Mr Ellis was dismissed from his post by the Archbishop of York the following year. We know not why, but Gibbon says "he probably got mixed up in the religious changes of the day by clinging too long to the old Catholic ways". He left in high dudgeon with "the instrument concerning the composition of the school" and in his will left this document with his executors until such time as a "worthy teachers should take the school in hand". What this document was we do not know, perhaps the decree restoring the salary from Toller's endowment, or regulations for the conduct of the school.

The civil war brought turbulence to the town and the school was closed either for the whole of the period between 1646 and 1649 or large parts of it. The building was used for housing troops and they can have had little respect for the place. Rents on the lands left for the upkeep of the school and property was siphoned off. Certainly the running of the school became chaotic and in 1654 Edward Browne was appointed the master by Lincoln College. Ermysted's these days is a model of harmonious organisation and efficiency but the problems of the master in those days are set out in a petition by the Lincoln College authorities who had put Browne in place to the Lords Commissioners of the Great Seal of England. The petition claimed that the assistant master (known as the usher) had abused the master and endangered his life, "a mad man very unable for that place, kept in, the lawful master by force of arms kept out", that tenants had refused to pay rents, rents had gone missing, the building was in disrepair and all sorts of unsavoury characters had their fingers in pies.

"The effect of their bloody oaths and cruel threats did manifest themselves by encouraging the usher – whose inability and unfitness have ruined the school – with some other loose persons to set upon the master in his said school, shut to the door and, as we are credibly informed, had undoubtedly slain him but he was rescued out of their hands," stated the petition which succeeded in its aim of securing an inquiry into the running of the school. The inquiry results are not known, Browne was no longer master in 1659 when John Collier took charge but the grammar school must have settled back into more settled ways. Old boy William Petyt went on to become Keeper of the Records in the Tower of London and a rich, influential gentleman in the corridors of power. Upon his death in 1707, his will he left £50 to the school and £200 for a scholarship to Christ's College, Cambridge. His brother, Sylvester, was also generous, and also left the vast sum of £30,000 to form the Petyt Trust, whose use was at first to provide piecemeal gifts to charities when thought fit but the large part of which was ultimately used in the 19th century to endow Skipton Girls' High School.

The gifts from the Petyt brothers occurred in the early part of the 18th century, but Gibbon describes this century as a "sorry picture of decay at the grammar school". He puts this down to the fact that, while rents were increasing, the costs were not. The churchwardens were interested only in the power of appointment while the masters were concerned with collecting rents and profits, in other words lining their pockets. These were interesting times. When the master Richard Leadal died in 1727 one of the applicants for the new post was John Wesley, the founder of Methodism. How different might the country's religious and social history have been had he been successful?

Wesley was at Lincoln College at the time, with its long-standing rights of appointment and was deemed to be a brilliant member. He wrote to his mother in March 1727 saying that he proposed to begin "an entirely different life with relation to the management of my expenses". He continued: "A school in Yorkshire, 40 miles from Doncaster, was proposed to me lately on which I shall think more about when it appears I may have it or not. A good salary is annexed to it; so that in a year's time tis probable all my debts would be paid. But what has made me wish for it most is the frightful description, as they call it, some gentlemen who know the place gave me of it yesterday. The town, Skipton-in-Craven, lies in a little vale so pent up between two hills that it is scarcely accessible on any side; so that you can expect little company from without and within there is none at all. I should therefore be entirely at liberty with company of my own choosing, whom for that reason I would bring with me." But Wesley's hopes were to be confounded, as the local electors in Skipton made their choice within the one month allowed them and they opted for a local man, William Banks, thus leaving Wesley to find an alternative means of settling his debts.

The master between 1730 and 1751, Matthew Wilkinson, joined when he was curate at Skipton but in 1732 he became vicar of Irthington, Cumberland, holding the living there until 1745. Quite how he combined these duties is unknown but upon his death the state of affairs grew even worse. For some time before his demise, Wilkinson had been ill and the jockeying for position as his successor had begun. The original £9 15s 4d of the Ermysted endowment had grown considerably as the rents had increased. Gibbon states that it was now worth at least £150 a year and probably a lot more. Two main candidates emerge, William West "a man of but moderate attainments" and Rev Stephen Barrett, an old boy and "a classical teacher of considerable eminence". West was offering bribes to the churchwardens for their vote, of £50 in some cases, a mere flask of whisky in others and Barrett was forced to compete although he seems to have been horrified. He wrote to the vicar of Carleton complaining that "I heartily pity all ye gentlemen of ye neighbourhood, yet it is in ye power of a parcel of venal rascals to put in any wretch yet will mount to their price". Barrett suggested that he would not be entering any auction for the forthcoming vacancy but when Wilkinson died he had changed his mind. A further letter to the Carleton vicar explains that he had been invited to dine with Lord Thanet where the vacancy was discussed, not least the prospect of having a man appointed who had not the skills necessary. Barrett agreed to pay, although he wanted no leak of his descent into corruption.

Barrett's party reckoned they had eight of the 12 votes sewn up but he himself was worried. Firstly, the churchwardens could change their minds if offered enough money and, secondly, they seemed far from unwilling to discuss the auction. Barrett, who was master of a school in Ashford, Kent, reckoned that giving up what must have been his reasonable living there for a more lucrative and likely but by no means certain position in Skipton withdrew. West, sensing which way the tide was running, also withdrew around the same time. With time running out on the churchwardens – and with it their chance of a nice little windfall - before the appointment passed into the hands of Lincoln College, two new candidates emerged. Rev George Chamberlain and Rev Thomas Carr of Bolton Abbey (who had been involved in the bribery by the two previous candidates). Fresh bribes were offered and the result was a six-six vote. Meanwhile rumours of the scandal were reaching Lincoln College, Oxford.

The situation then descended into sheer farce. Carr took matters into his own hands, entered the school and started teaching. Three weeks later a Rev Samuel Plomer arrived, claiming to be the new head appointed by Lincoln College. Carr's response was to close the school, lock all the doors and batten down the hatches for a siege. He was to claim that Plomer had tried several clandestine ways to gain entry and even used violence and the school was closed from November 1751 to the summer of 1752. The assistant master, Mr Colton, must have enjoyed the situation. Carr raised his salary from £25 to £40, plied him with liquor and he had no-one to teach! How this intriguing situation was resolved is not recorded but it was Plomer who emerged triumphant – perhaps pressure was put on Carr by the locals who could see no way out.

A few more details are worth adding to the story of Mr Plomer, who came to the school in such extraordinary circumstances. He was to play a part in several notable episodes in the town's history and generally concerned himself with much of the town's affairs. It is intriguing to note that Plomer was extremely interested in agriculture (his clerk was to write to the new canal company complaining that they were not keeping the fences in proper order and his cattle were breaking loose) and the son of his old adversary, Thomas Carr, was the breeder of the famous Craven Heifer calf whose name adorns so many pubs in the district and whose painting adorned those early Craven Bank notes. Plomer was also one of those who challenged, unsuccessfully, the Castle's monopoly in grinding corn and its right to "soke money" described in an earlier chapter. He also was petitioner for the enclosure of the Tarn Moor, an area to the north of the town which now includes the Craven Heifer pub and land alongside the bypass. This open land was common land but in 1767 an Act of Parliament allowed it to be enclosed and handed over to a body of trustees (which included those notorious churchwardens!). The land was then rented out and the income used for the relief of the poor and the Poor Rate (a local tax used to prevent the destitute of the area from starving). He was a trustee of the Keighley to Kendal turnpike road and also sold two acres of land to the west of the school along which the canal was to pass (and along which the Millennium Walk passes). Plomer died in 1780, much respected and was succeeded by his old adversary, Thomas Carr. Gibbon's book is fairly positive that he had been promised the position after Plomer as a sweetener for ending his occupation of the school back in 1752, pointing out that this was the only recorded unanimous decision by the churchwardens before 1793 and it was difficult to see the electors selecting a man of such advanced years, for those times, of 50 (the Prime Minister of the time was 24).

If the Plomer v Carr battle was a low point, it was not the abyss. The school had no reason to be a success. The master received an income and his personal wealth depended upon how much of that he spent on the upkeep of the school. The fewer scholars, the more he could keep in his pocket. Gibbon cites evidence that while the school taught Latin, Scripture and English according to its foundation charter, writing and arithmetic were "extras" and there was a charge. Typical of the old endowed schools in the country, writes Gibbon, Ermysted's had drifted into "uselessness, inefficiency and corruption" and speaks of "an amazing story of decay". Little wonder that other schools were springing up. Meanwhile when Carr died in 1792 four men came forward eager to secure the very handy sum of £320 a year which the headship was worth.

They were Rev William Carr, son of the previous incumbent, Rev Richard Withnell, curate at Holy Trinity, Rev John Coates and Rev J Heelis son of Lord Thanet's agent at the castle.

The battle to secure the headmastership of the school after Carr was even more sordid than what went on before and Gibbon records it honestly in his history. Rev Withnell was straight out of the starting blocks. He had the support of the vicar, Rev T Marsden, who seems to have been anxious to promote him away from his curacy at the parish church (thus saving about £30 a year by employing a younger, inexperienced, curate). On the very day that Carr died, Withnell had a nomination form signed by the vicar and hurried round the church wardens and that night, in a public house at Halton East owned by one of the wardens, six of them met to plot his election. One of the wardens, Thomas Ianson, is alleged to have said that Rev Coates had promised £100 for a vote but Withnell had "promised that sum or more to six of us". With seven votes already in the bag, a meeting was swiftly called and as each of the 12 electors arrived at the vestry he was presented with a notice which stated: "Sirs, I do hereby require and demand of you to induct me in possession of the Free Grammar School in Skipton of which I am appointed schoolmaster. Signed Richard Withnell". A stormy meeting followed but Withnell was voted in with the other five churchwardens signing a protest in the vestry book.

The keys to the school were in the hands of the Earl of Thanet at Skipton Castle and his agent, whose son of course was a rival candidate, refused to hand them over. Undaunted the vicar and three other churchwardens found themselves a locksmith and broke into the school, sparking another protest in the vestry book. Withnell hurried off to York to secure a licence to teach from the Archbishop, who claimed the right to examine the new headmaster's religion, morals and learning. Withnell refused, the Archbishop persisted and the curate headed back to Skipton without his licence. News of the scandal had by now reached Lincoln College and once again they were none too pleased. They appointed their own candidate, Rev William Bright, who had the misfortune of dying before he could set out for Skipton!

Withnell's party then called another meeting, hoping to add legitimacy to their claim by winning a second, "free" election. But here one of their party, John Ward, appears to have been having second thoughts or upping the price of his vote. The vicar "in a violent passion, with a paper in his hand and with a loud, threatening voice" demanded that Ward should sign. He would not back down and Gibbon, whose research is based on documents in the "School Chest", claims that after the meeting had broken up Ward was finally persuaded to sign the nomination form but only after he had been plied with drink. Lincoln College though was not to be fobbed off so easily and put forward their new nominee, Rev Thomas Gartham. The matter was in the hands of lawyers and the school was closed down while the wheels of justice turned. They turned in favour of Withnell, a judge ruling that he had been rightfully elected by a majority vote but there remained one obstacle – the licence required from the Archbishop. It seems that Withnell's qualifications must have been at best dubious for he again refused to put himself to the test and again the lawyers were called in. The case was heard in front of the King's Bench and was of great importance for it would decide whether the whole system of licensing teachers could be enforced or whether examination was scrapped. Lord Chief Justice, Lord Kenyon, ruled against Withnell and, after a closure period of four years, the school was reopened in 1796, under the headmastership of Rev Gartham.

Gartham was in office but it must have been an awkward situation, given that Withnell, the vicar and the churchwardens were still on the scene. And Gartham appears to have been no high-minded moralist. He immediately demanded four years back pay (needless to say to no success) and sold off limestone and timber to a total value of £310, pocketing the proceeds. In 1799 legal proceedings were started in which some of the churchwardens claimed that Gartham had let lands to himself at a very high price (the point being that as he paid the rent to himself, he was able to fend off others who wanted the land and sub let it to his own substantial profit). While an action was filed, it appears not to have been heard but the incident shows the bitterness and the corruption surrounding Ermysted's.

More battles and a revival

A NEW vicar arrived in 1806, Rev John Peering but the battle with Gartham showed no sign of abating. It festered for several years and came to a head in 1822 when a public meeting was called at the Black Horse to "consider the best means to be adopted for rendering the said school a useful and efficient establishment". From it emerged a vicious attack on Gartham, displayed publicly in the shop of John Tasker, bookseller (the same man who founded the Craven

Herald) and later in the auction room of John Merryweather for signature. The petition stated "For 20 years the inhabitants of the parish have been deprived of the benefit they ought to have derived from the school owing to the gross, immoral character of the present master who was an improper person to be entrusted with the education of children". It claimed that £5,000 had been spent by locals sending their boys off to other schools because the Free Grammar School was not a fit place. Other allegations were that he had held auction sales "collecting multitudes of disorderly people under the pretence of offering buildings for sale", that he had been arrested for debt (there is no evidence for this; Gartham claimed he had been framed and there was a rumour that he only dare leave the school on Sundays as this was the one day he could not be arrested for debt), that he had eccentric ideas on teaching, that he offered himself for marriage to daughters of some townsfolk without any previous acquaintance, that he failed to keep the school open at the proper times (the school bell having found its way to the Black Horse) and that he treated the vicar and churchwardens with derision.

What a catalogue of invective! What a hotbed of gossip the town must have been in 1822! A story was that when the vicar did come to inspect the school, Gartham challenged him to a debate in Latin in front of the boys and called for a spelling book for one of the wardens. This perhaps explains the derision charge but what, if anything lay behind those juicy tales of proposing marriage to all and sundry?

Another interesting point in this thoroughly libellous petition was the charge that there were only 16 scholars at the school and 14 of these were "children of persons in humble stations of life", an accusation positively reeking of snobbery. They were, it was claimed, being paid to attend to ensure the continuation of the school. Whether or not the school bell had found its way into the pub is also unclear but a new school bell was acquired in 1829, augmented by a bugle! (In 1909 Lord Hothfield presented the Old Market Cross bell to the school and it is still in service today).

Faced with the petition the churchwardens and vicar sacked Gartham. To no one's surprise he refused to go, appealing to the Earl of Thanet who refused to intervene. The church party's next move was to appoint his successor, a curate at the church, Rev Robert Thomlinson and they turned up at the school and broke in when Gartham refused to leave. A large crowd was gathering to witness these extraordinary scenes and the ousted master obviously had his supporters as they forced open the doors again, kicked out the vicar and the churchwardens and reinstated Mr Gartham.

The lawyers were active again, the notable Henry Alcock acting for the church party. At York it was ruled that Gartham had to leave but only subject to a decision in the Court of Common Pleas in London that the dismissal was valid. Gartham argued that since no reason had been specified in the legal action, he had been unable to defend himself and the aforementioned Court agreed with him, the dismissal was ruled wrongful. Thus Ermysted's was in the hands of a master hated by his nominal employers, locked in, refusing to leave while little was said of the education being delivered. At least the tenants of the school lands were happy. Uncertain as to who was in control, they simply withheld their rents.

The vicar and wardens gathered evidence to justify the dismissal on the grounds that the conditions of the Foundation deed such as hours of schooling etc and mentioned above were not being followed. A meeting was held in the vestry (where the vicar complained of being subjected to "scurrilous abuse" by Gartham) was not a success. Witnesses such as the former assistant John Wade claimed he had kept to the regulations and Wade spoke of a Friday night class for children of both sexes for which Gartham had provided books and candles at his own expense. Thomlinson however claimed immorality (Gartham had not been to church for 20 days), neglect (the gardens and orchards had been stripped) and delinquency.

One cannot help but feel that the strain on Gartham must have contributed to his death in December of 1824, still in possession. It brought an end to the strife. Such a wonderful story of gossip, local politics and a power struggle may seem incredible to the modern reader, but a read of Charles Dickens, writing a couple of decades later, shows that the tribulations in Skipton may not have been so unusual. Gartham's death enabled the smooth transition of Robert Thomlinson to the post.

By 1841 Ermysted's was facing increased competition for its services. A National School (one which received grants from the Church of England provided it followed the teachings of the church, ie was not Nonconformist) had opened in 1814 on Rectory Lane today the site of the Three Links Club). Ermysted's brought in a new constitution and the school room was enlarged (the shape of the original and the extended walls can clearly be seen later in the old building, later in the walk). Also amended were the school hours, to a less draconian 8am to noon and 2pm to 5pm. The school was also caught up in debate over the usefulness of Latin. There were those who argued that English and mathematics were more important matters, others who said that the provision of Latin ensured that it was distinct from a National School, patronised by the lowest classes of society.

In 1869 a report by the Schools Inquiry Commission painted a very different picture from the glowing Ofsted (Office for Standards in Education) report which the school was to receive in 1997. The school numbers were given as 45, with only 36 in attendance on the day of inspection. The inspector stated: "I found some difficulty in examining the scholars owing to the extreme disorder and the absence of any proper classification. The boys did not seem to know their classes or to have any system as to the prosecution of work...on the whole the instruction of the school appeared to me to be slovenly, immethodical and unintelligent and I could find no one subject in which the boys seemed to take an interest or which had been taught with average care or success. This may be partially accounted for by the state of the discipline, which is evidently most inefficient".

Ermysted's was at its lowest ebb. Numbers were pitifully poor and closure was just round the corner. Other grammar schools in the neighbourhood – Burnsall, Kirkby Malham, Earby and Bolton Abbey were to cease to function as such in the early 1870s and became elementary schools. Ermysted's, perhaps in an act of desperation, decided on radical changes. The rule of the churchwardens was to come to an end, to be replaced by a body of governors, drawn from public life, in control of the school's still extensive estate. The headmaster no longer needed to be a cleric nor a graduate of Oxford or Cambridge. Fees (no less than £3, no more than £6 a year) introduced with scholarships for those who passed an entrance examination. Thus the school was to be no longer a Free Grammar School. Most importantly, the school was to move to new premises and take in boarders at a new site it owned off Gargrave Road.

The move, which eventually took place in 1876 under a new headmaster, Edward Hartley, who took just 13 boys from the Newmarket Street site and recruited another 13. In his first speech day he freely admitted that the school certainly did not have a good name when he came to it but with his hand on the tiller, the school flourished. Its extensive dormitories for the boarders were a revelation and it certainly was a major change from the old, cramped rooms on Newmarket Street. The school disposed of many lands to finance its move to such spacious premises. The Old Grammar School site went for £2,364, land at

Eastby for £5,149, various land in Skipton and Addingham for £6,350 and land near the railway station for £6,350. Even so, times were hard balancing the books. A letter to the Craven Pioneer of September 1874, before the move to Gargrave Road, bemoaned the introduction of fees. Under the nom-de-plume of "Working Man", the author told how that after deductions every day he had less than three and a halfpence to feed and clothe his family. Consequently, much as he would like to, he would not be sending his son to the grammar school and it was no surprise that its numbers were declining.

Even so Hartley is greatly praised for his work in establishing the school not just academically but physically. He is credited with planting the great trees which form its impressive frontage. He was to resign in 1907, supposedly disillusioned with growing interference in the running of an independent school. Certainly by the time of his departure, old boys in large numbers were achieving scholarships to Oxford, Cambridge and other universities and going on to important posts in medicine, education and science.

The 20th century history of Ermysted's has been one of progress and success. The juicy tales of rows and strife are long gone. Major structural additions were made in 1933, 1959 and 1971. The Education Act of 1944 turned Ermysted's into a voluntary aided school, which removed fees and gave the local education authority some say in the running of the school. In 1992 a visit by Ann, Princess Royal, marked the 500th anniversary of the death of Peter Toller and two years later an appeal for funds to build a Sports Hall on site was brought to a successful conclusion. Boarding had ceased in 1989 under the headmastership of David Buckroyd but now it caters for more than 600 pupils. The competition for places is fierce.

7: Workhouse and hospital

The Walk continues along to the end of Park Avenue, opposite Ermysted's, and then turns left into Brook Street.

At the end of Park Avenue one may just catch a glimpse, a little further along Gargrave Road, on the right and next to the relatively new hall at Ermysted's School, the old Skipton workhouse. This was built in 1840 at a cost of £6,000 to replace an earlier workhouse established in a former dyehouse off the Keighley Road. The Poor Law Act required local authorities to provide for relief of the destitute. The building is a grade II listed building and was transformed in 1995 into a housing complex. The workhouse provided a roof for the elderly or incapacitated members of society and it also supplied food and lodgings for itinerants. However, as readers of Oliver Twist will remember, it was far from a benevolent institution. Our Victorian forebears believed that too easy a life would encourage indolence and conditions were harsh, rules rigid. A Board of Guardians ran the workhouse from the public purse and were keen not to waste money,

Craven Herald reports of the Board of Guardian meetings suggest that it was more akin to a prison, although conditions were improving at the turn of the century. Certainly, the elderly attempted to accrue savings to avoid ending their days in the workhouse. In June 1897 the Herald reported that the medical officer of the workhouse was concerned about the diet of patients, which he complained was being interfered with by friends bringing in unsuitable food and wanted a ban on such gifts. He also complained at the lack of a separate ward to deal with lunatics and "noisy cases". The Queen's diamond jubilee that year also caused some debate among the Board members. A number were teetotallers and they decided, somewhat peevishly, to ban alcohol from the inmates' special jubilee celebration lunch of lamb and peas. The Herald noted however that the Guardians were allowed to choose between a glass of Bass ale or Guinness stout! Maybe the barb struck home for later that year the Board met and agreed to allow the officers the discretion to allow beer and spirits to be consumed at the Christmas dinner, but only by a vote of 18-15. It was stated that alcohol had been allowed in the past with no record of drunken behaviour.

Another Herald report from the time stated how a woman had been reported to the Society for the Prevention of Cruelty to Children. Discharged from the workhouse in November 1897 the woman, of Union Square, returned five times in an intoxicated state with her four children, one of them an infant in her arms, drenched in the rain. Justice was swift for she was in court the following week and jailed for three months, her children being sent to the workhouse. The woman, who worked at Mr Sidgwick's High Mill, told the court that she was treated violently by her husband and had been forced to tramp the countryside.

After the inception of the NHS in 1948, the site became a hospital for the elderly and also had two wards for general medical patients. In later years Alfred Walker was the master and his wife Mary the matron; they died in the late 1970s. Both are remembered with respect, indeed affection, in the town. Both were awarded the Queen's Jubilee Medal in 1977. Alf became administrator around 1939 and his wife was to remain matron until the 1960s and they transformed the hospital, which had been very much for the poor and itinerant. The Walkers' endeavours turned it into a comfortable home for the elderly, food was improved and Mrs Walker allowed such luxuries as female patients having their hair trimmed. After it came under NHS control there were wards for acute and chronic medical patients as well as the elderly but the medical wards ceased in the mid-1970s and thereafter Raikeswood was solely for the elderly. Norman Hodgson, a founder member of the Friends of Skipton Hospital in 1948, told an amusing story of how the first television was brought on to the wards as a result of the Friends' fund raising efforts the first programme to be shown was a cricket match, which led to an elderly patient complaining about the "boys next door at Ermysted's playing too close to the windows". The hospital was closed in 1991, with considerable local resentment.

Turn left into Brook Street

Somewhere along Brook Street was the route of Skipton's first railway. A simple system of rope and pulley hauled small wagons from an unloading point at the canal to a stone quarry which was later handily adapted to form the tennis courts at Skipton Girls' High School. Once loaded the wagons were returned to the canal basin for transportation.

As Brook Street bends to the right, don't miss the unusual view above Skipton, particularly of the award-winning Union Mill development, which our walk does not pass. This was supposedly the roughest part of the town. The Police had to patrol these area in twos as a minimum. It was here that the casual labourers would lodge. An elderly Skipton woman, committing her memories to audiotape for Craven Museum in the 1990s, said: "When I was a young girl a boy might ask to see me home from a dance, until he found out I lived in Union Square. Tough though they were they were kind and generous people."

At this point to the right, up the hill, is the site of the first Skipton and District Hospital, built on the corner of Brook Street and Granville Street in 1901. To mark the Diamond Jubilee of Queen Victoria in 1897 there was a meeting of the townsfolk to decide upon a fitting project and the hospital was chosen in preference to a public library. It was a remarkably popular scheme and the funds were raised without difficulty by public subscription. Lord Hothfield was the chief benefactor. The site was worth £680 but he sold it for £500 and promised to return £350 of that as a donation when it was completed. Known as the Cottage Hospital, the foundation stone was laid by Lord Hothfield in 1898 and Lady Frederick Cavendish opened the hospital a year later and the secretary was none other than William Harbutt Dawson, the author of the most extensive history of Skipton. Writing in 1946, Dawson, by now well into his 80s, wrote: "Costly though the maintenance of the hospital proved, its income from the first kept abreast with the ever-increasing expenditure."

In 1932, outgrowing its premises, the hospital was moved to Whinfield on Keighley Road and previously the home of Tom Fattorini, the famous jeweller. The newer hospital, at Whinfield, is now known as Skipton General Hospital. Now it is used for outpatients and the Physical Rehabilitation Unit. The main hospital in the area, Airedale General Hospital, was opened in 1970. All trace of the Cottage Hospital is now gone and houses have been built on that site.

Also up the hill, past the new houses on the site of the old hospital, are the administrative headquarters of Craven District Council, the local authority for Skipton and the southern part of the Yorkshire Dales.

Continue along Brook Street down the hill and cross the swing bridge of the canal

At this point one is confronted by the imposing structure of Dewhurst's Mill on the right, and the old brewery on the left. Scott's brewery has long gone but its private water supply, from Massa Flatts near the workhouse, can still be traced. Little is known of the brewery which appears to have closed when taken over by Bentley's Brewery soon after the First World War.

8: Mills and textiles

The Walk has now crossed the canal. To the left is the redeveloped Union Mill and the town centre. A short diversion to left will offer a view into the award winning Victoria Mill, Bellmont Wharfe redevelopment. These are certainly not the worst slums in England. Eller Beck passes under the canal and heads southwards to the Aire. Immediately on the right is Dewhurst's Mill. It seems an appropriate time to review the story of Skipton's mills.

For more than a century textiles were Skipton's major employer but when cheaper foreign imports came to flood the market its decline was rapid. It took barely 20 years, from the 1960s to the 1980s for textiles to go from chief employer to virtually non-existent.

Dewhurst's Mill still dominates the town but its textile days are now long gone. As late as the 1970s Dewhurst's famous "Sew it with Sylko" slogan was a familiar sight in households and wooden bobbins with cotton thread in all sorts of colours were a feature of households across the land. The slogan was written in huge letters across a walkway above Broughton Road which connected the mill with its store sheds on the opposite side of the road.

The mill, was opened by a cotton spinner operating in the vicinity of Skipton, John Dewhurst, in 1828 producing worsted yarns on land bought from the heirs of William Chamberlain, a merchant who owned extensive land on the west side of the town. Dewhurst was to show the vision which was to single out his firm as the leading manufacturer in the town by being the first to introduce power looms in 1829, although Dawson notes that he took the precaution of bringing them in with absolute secrecy and securely boxed up so that most would not know what was in the crates. In 1831 the mill burnt down - possibly as a result of arson - but was rebuilt and operating again within six months. Further trouble was to visit Mr Dewhurst again in 1842 with a visit of rioters protesting against new technology putting them out of jobs (the incident is dealt with in greater detail in chapter 10) .

However the firm prospered and the Craven Herald of December 1854 was able to report on the addition of a weaving shed and 385 looms. A special celebration was held at the Craven Hotel for all the workers but John Dewhurst was presented by illness from attending, the business now being under the control of his son, John Bonny Dewhurst. Another misfortune was to strike when civil war broke out in the United States of America. So effective was the blockade by the Northern Union states on the ports of the southern Confederate states, thus cutting off the supply of cotton, that there was a very real threat of Great Britain entering the war on the Confederate side. The Craven Pioneer was to write in October 1874: "During the American war the trade of Skipton like that of most towns in Lancashire and Yorkshire where cotton spinning and weaving is the staple trade was materially affected and even in 1866, after the declaration of peace it had not revived. Business seemed to languish and the prospects were far from promising to our trades people".

The Dewhursts were a typical enterprising Victorian commercial family and they diversified into cotton threads treated with sodium hydroxide which produced a lustre. Thus cheap cotton could replace spun silk and this seems to have given rise to the name of Sylko, a combination of the words silk and cotton. The depression of the Civil War was short lived. A new and large mill was built, occupying five stories, on Broughton Road on February 4 1870. The entire premises occupied 20,000 square yards and between 800 and 900 people worked there. An article in the Craven Pioneer of October 1874, written by an unnamed Fellow of the Royal Astronomical Society describes the new factory: "The rooms are large and lofty, they are also well lighted and ventilated, every attention being paid to the health and comfort of the 800 work people employed in both mills. So far as is practicable, all moving portions of machinery are covered or supplied with guards so as to prevent accidents. This is done so thoroughly that it is impossible for any accident to arise from machinery except by carelessness."

The Dewhursts were for many years the largest single employer in the town, John Bonny Dewhurst and his family moved into Aireville Park and lived the life of magnates. In 1897 the Dewhursts joined forces with 14 other English firms to form the English Sewing Company (also included was Rickards Mill at Bell Busk and Skipton. The Dewhurst control of their empire was to fade however, their building continued to be known as Dewhurst's mill and still is today.

The firm continued to be a symbol of Skipton's wealth and it came as something of a shock, despite the obvious decline of the British textile industry, when the English Sewing Company announced in February 1983 the closure of its Skipton operations in August of that year. When the mill closed the premises were taken over by Kingsley Cards, manufacturers of birthday and greetings cards. In 1993 the old mill chimney, a major landmark in the town, was demolished due to the high costs of insurance and maintenance. It was another link with the town's 19th century textile expansion severed.

While Dewhurst's was the major textile manufacturer in Skipton, it was by no means the first. When Robert de Clifford came into possession of the castle and honour of Skipton at the beginning of the 14th century, there was already a fulling mill in the town. Tax returns and parish registers show the presence of dyers, felt makers, linen makers, weavers and wool combers through the 17th and 18th centuries. Hand loom weaving was an important industry by 1800 - indeed the houses forming Union Square were built with special accommodation for hand loom weavers. Each house was furnished with two stories above the ground floor, the top room being intended as a work room.

The oldest mill in Skipton was the High Mill in Castle Woods built in 1785 for the seventh Earl of Thanet and a lease was granted a lease to Peter Garforth, John Blackburn and John Sidgwick. The mill produced cotton yarns but not without problems for, in 1786 the mill was stopped for a time because of a legal action in which it was claimed that equipment was a copy of Richard Arkwright's water powered looms and thus a breach of patent. The action was unsuccessful and by 1806 Sidgwick was the sole lessee and his family was to run the firm and their name crops up regularly in the life of Skipton. Water powered from the start, steam power was introduced in 1820 and in 1839 the Sidgwicks also built Low Mill on the canal side off Sackville Street where weaving and weft spinning was carried out. However, the Sidgwicks were not as competent in keeping on top of the latest innovations. Although they employed 238 people in 1881, the firm could not compete with the large scale units springing up in Lancashire and in 1890 Sidgwicks closed and much of the High Mill was demolished. Low Mill was purchased by CA Rickards of Bell Busk, part of the English Sewing Company combine and continued to produce silk thread for hand and sewing machinery and for weaving silk.

Disaster was to strike in November 1908 during the night shift when a piece of silk that dropped on to naked flame of a lamp, held by one Walker Taylor of Castle Street, flared up. That set fire to an oil soaked driving belt and within minutes the whole building was on fire. The roof fell in and the interior was gutted and more than 300 people lost their jobs. Sackville Mill was built on the site in 1914 and in 1996 it was demolished to make way for housing.

Textile production really took off in the second half of the 19th century. Until that time the town was hampered by the refusal of the Earls of Thanet to allow land to be released for development - though perhaps modern Skiptonians have cause to be grateful to the owner of Skipton Castle. Without their restraining hand it is feasible that Skipton would have expanded in much the same way as other West Riding textile towns, for example Keighley, did in the first half of the Industrial Revolution. Titus Salt came to Skipton to acquire a site around Caroline Square for his Victorian mills but was discouraged by the attitude of the castle estate. Unable to buy or acquire land on a long lease he headed south to build the Victorian village of Saltaire, now a world heritage site. The vast Salts Mill, home now of ultra-modern company Pace, manufacturing digital television components, might have been situated in Skipton.

While the Earl, as we have seen, paid for the development of High Mill in Skipton Woods, he was determined to control the extent of development. Land was not released except on short leases, typically 40 or 50 years, with no freehold sales thus deterring any potential entrepreneur. The last Earl of Thanet, the 11th, died in 1849 without an heir and his Skipton estates passed to Sir Richard Tufton, who was created a baronet in 1851. Sir Richard was persuaded by his agent, Angus Nicholson, to depart from the earls' policy and both the freehold disposal of land and 99 year leases became common. However, the Tuftons were absentee landlords, residing in Kent and even in 1875 the Pioneer was to write of Sir Henry Tufton (later Lord Hothfield): "As a natural leader in the neighbourhood we think he fails to secure for himself that respect and to make his influence felt to the extent which he might do if he came more frequently. Property has duties as well as rights."

Nevertheless, the Tuftons, prompted by Angus Nicholson released land, principally for the building of Middletown and Newtown. The Craven Herald obituary for Nicholson reads: "It was solely due to his persistent exertions that the castle authorities were persuaded to extend the term for which leasehold land was sold from 60 to 99 years and it was chiefly owing to his efforts also that the traditional unwillingness to sell freehold property was overcome."

The first mill to be built after this relaxation was Union Shed, situated off Keighley Road on the banks of the canal in 1867. This was financed by local speculators offering room and power and housed small tenants. A similar venture was opened in 1897 off Broughton Road. These small operators appear to have flourished. Samuel Farey, for example, had come to Skipton in 1844 in order to take up a post as headmaster of the British School but in 1866 he left and by 1871 was a weaver at Union Shed. His change of career proved a great success and in 1878 he opened Firth Mill on Sackville Street where he and his son operated until 1925. The Firth Mill was then taken over by Mark Nutter, who produced rayon umbrella material until closure in 1970. During the war Nutter's produced parachute material with coloured sewing – there so that if the parachute failed the War Ministry would know which firm was responsible.

George Walton, another graduate of Union Shed, built Alexandra Shed off Keighley Road (demolished in 1982) while John Wilkinson built Park Shed on Brougham Street, near its junction with Newmarket Street and also mills in Lancashire employing more than 1,000 workers. Union Shed eventually came to be the possession of one firm, Smith Hartley, which had moved there from Linton in 1878 and then gradually swallowed up other operators until it ceased trading in 1980. A similar thing happened at Broughton Road, where Rycroft and Hartley were dominant until fire destroyed most of the premises in 1958. At the time of writing Union Shed is being converted into dwellings, after serving some years as home to a range of small businesses while the remnants of the Broughton Road mill are now being used as a warehouse.

As the textile trade expanded rapidly, so too did the population of Skipton. The census of 1831, 1841 and 1851 show a static population (4,842 rising to 5,044 and then falling again to 4,962). There was then a steady rise - 5,451 in 1861 and 6,078 in 1861 - before a huge leap, to 9,091 in 1881 and 10,376 in 1891. A peak was reached in 1911 at 12,977, when textile production was at its height. Since then the population has been virtually static as the textile industry declined and new industries took its place. The 1991 census showed a population for the town of 13,533.

Alas post World War Two the mills of Skipton have entered into a terminal decline. Only Mason's textiles, which specialises in such things as ties, remains, but on a new site off Carleton Road. Cheaper foreign imports did the damage with the closure of the English Sewing Company (better known as Dewhurst's in the town) coming as a severe blow to the morale of the town.

9: Railways

From the swing bridge across the canal, continue along the towpath to the next swing bridge

The walk then heads out of town along the canal. It passes on the left Herriot's Hotel, which began life as the Midland Hotel, catering for passengers from the railway station opposite It was severely damaged by fire in 1918 and rebuilt. The swing bridge forms the southern entrance to Aireville Park. This large open area was acquired by the town council at the end of the Second World War and is widely used by Skiptonians and visitors today. Originally it was the grounds of a large house built for the lawyer Henry Alcock, Aireville Grange. Upon Alcock's death in 1869 it was taken over by the mill owner John Bonney Dewhurst and the house and gardens remained in that family's possession as a private residence and grounds. During World War Two Aireville Grange was requisitioned by the War Department and the parkland was used for training purposes. In 1945 West Yorkshire County Council's education authority took over the hall and, after much debate over its future, it subsequently became Aireville County Secondary School. Aireville School was formally opened in 1958 by Iain McLeod and since then has undergone several extensions.

Meanwhile the grounds were bought by the town from the Dewhurst family and opened to the public. They have long been popular for a variety of pursuits, most notably the Skipton Gala, which in 1999 celebrated its centenary.

The large open parkland, situated in a natural amphitheatre, serves as the destination of the floats and procession, base for a fairground and site of events. At the north eastern corner of the park, on Gargrave Road, stand war memorial gates in memory of those Skiptonians who died in the Second World War. It was dedicated in 1956. One of the finest pitch and putt golf courses in the country is sited at the western end of the park. Opened in July 1969 it was further improved in 1999 as part of a general project for refurbishing the park with money from the Millennium Commission.

Aireville is also home to the town's swimming pool, opened in March 1964 by the Olympic swimmer Anita Lonsborough. This was not without controversy either as it is a 33 and a third yard long pool, a distance which was obsolete for competitive swimming almost as soon as it was opened. In the mid-1990s maintenance costs for the pool due to inherent building defects had escalated to such an extent that Craven District Council sought Lottery grants to rebuild the swimming pool. At the time of writing the future of the pool is unsure.

Those who wish may cross the swing bridge to sample the park's charms. Or, to continue the walk, turn left down the hill towards the railway station. Take extreme care crossing the road at an awkward road junction and walk across the car park into the top left hand corner for the entrance to a narrow walkway which leads along the main railway line.

On the left is the front of Herriot's and opposite used to be situated the Skipton rail station master's house but that was knocked down and replaced by the fire station upon the reorganisation of local government in 1974. What is now an amusing tale from 1974 relates how the firemen took delivery of a brand new engine, only to write it off on virtually its first mission en route to a barn fire near Grassington, when it took the hump back bridge at Threshfield a little too briskly, left the road and demolished a telegraph pole and 60 yards of dry stone wall.

To the right is the Carleton New Road, which turns 90 degrees to the left to form a bridge over the Broughton Road (the old road to Lancashire). This bridge was constructed in 1888 to take the place of a level crossing.

A visitor to Skipton railway station at the start of the new Millennium cannot fail to be impressed by its tidy and pleasing appearance. It was not always the case. Indeed, less than 10 years previously, Skipton had that all too familiar air of decline and forthcoming closure which was the hallmark of British Rail. The privatisation of Britain's rail network may not have been the cause of the revival – it is for others to argue the case one way or another – but it was certainly contemporaneous. A large sum was spent on restoring Skipton railway station to its former glories and a plaque alongside the main platform announces the official re-opening by Sir Alfred McAlpine to mark the 150th anniversary of the opening of the line to Skipton. While there is room for improvement – the club outside the entrance, for example, is hardly an attractive welcome to the modern rail traveller – the station has the look of a thriving provincial station. Indeed, with twice hourly trains to Leeds and Bradford and a daily direct service to London (brought back in 1998 after an absence of more than 25 years), Skiptonians are returning to their rail service in ever increasing numbers. Another advantage has been the growth in popularity of the Settle to Carlisle line (which as late as 1989 was threatened with closure). At the time of writing rail lines to Skipton could look forward to even more traffic with plans announced to restore the old line to Grassington as a rail route to Swinden, near Cracoe, where it now terminates at Tilcon's quarry and to link the Embsay and Bolton Abbey railway, a steam line, to the main network near Embsay. And in October 1999 the Leeds to Glasgow direct line via Skipton was re-started, another sign of the growing confidence in rail travel.

The current railway station is, however, not the original. That was situated a little south of the current building, on the site of the current Tesco supermarket. It was from here that passenger traffic started on September 7 1847 on the line constructed by the Leeds and Bradford Railway Company, which reached Keighley in March 1847, Skipton in the September and Colne, where it linked up with the East Lancashire Railway, in October 1848. Six days earlier, on September 1 1847, a special train carried the railway company's directors and guests, who included Sir Matthew Wilson, of High Street statue fame, to the town. Cheering crowds thronged the route from Keighley and, upon arrival in the town, a band led a procession to a banquet and entertainment held at the Devonshire Hotel before the train returned to Leeds at 8pm.

It was not long before the complaints about the station started. The Craven Herald in 1857 carried a complaint about the lack of covered waiting accommodation on the North bound platform. The Leeds Mercury in 1873 stated: "There is but one waiting room about 16 feet square for all male passengers and on market days especially this is crowded with cattle drovers and sometimes their dogs, butchers etc and as the men are frequently 'the worse for drink' the first and second class passengers are 'left out in the cold'. As there is no refreshment room at the station, the evil is more serious".

By now the line was owned by the Midland Railway and was becoming increasingly busy. Rail links had been established with Morecambe to take hard working West Riding folk on well earned trips to the seaside. These were also popular from Skipton, as advertisements and indeed reports in the local press indicate. The Midland Railway, in bitter rivalry with other competing services, particularly for a route to Scotland, had been experiencing difficulties in connections with the London and North Western route at Ingleton. The aim seems to have been to make it as difficult as possible to catch a connecting service to Scotland using Midland routes. So it was that the Midland built the Settle to Carlisle route and a new station at Skipton was opened on April 30 1876, the day before passenger services started on the new Settle-Carlisle line.

The competition among the early railway companies was illustrated by the Select Committee of the House of Lords which met in May 1882 to hear the arguments for a Bill allowing the Skipton and Ilkley Railway Company to build a line linking the two towns and to which the main objector was the Midland Railway Company. It feared a link up with big rivals, the North Eastern Railway Company, and thus an encroachment into Midland territory. In fact, the Skipton and Ilkley Company reached an agreement in which they withdrew their bill on condition that the Midland would introduce their own within 12 months with a view to completing the line by 1888. If the Midland failed to do so, the original promoters were entitled to reintroduce their original bill and the Midland would not oppose it and would also construct the line at their own expense. Matters started but the Midland seemed reluctant to press ahead. An article in the Craven Herald of 1885 reminded them of their agreement and in April it reported that a contract for the building of a line had been awarded to a Bristol company, Mousley and Co.

The line was not an easy construction. The route swings off and swiftly crosses both the canal and the Keighley Road before heading towards Embsay, climbing steeply and requiring embankments and bridges as it cuts through the Middletown and Otley Road areas of the town. It is this route which will link the Embsay and Bolton Abbey Steam Railway to the network should ambitious plans come to fruition in the new Millennium (alas the route beyond Bolton Abbey has been ripped up and built over).

One further line was to be established from Skipton - north to Grassington. There were several schemes put forward in the second half of the 19th century for such a route, all taking in a route via Flasby and Hetton and assuming a link over (and under) the Dales to the north east. It was not until 1897 that the Yorkshire Dales Railway Company, under the chairmanship of Sir Matthew Wilson, obtained approval for a line which would spur off from the Skipton to Ilkley route. The line's propagandists argued that the route would boost tourism, attract commuters to the villages en route, boost the quarry industry and revive the dying lead mines around Grassington. The first sod was cut on June 7 1900 by MP Walter Morrison (readers may remember that he was Wilson's great political rival, particularly in the affair of the High Street statue) and the line itself opened on July 28 1902. A special train left Skipton four minutes late (due to the delay of a connecting train carrying guests) and once again residents along the line turned out to cheer the new spectacle. The line terminated at Grassington station, which in fact was situated at Threshfield, it being too expensive to build a viaduct across the relatively deep gorge of the river Wharfe.

By now Skipton's railway links were at their zenith and the industry played an important role in the economy of the town. The census of 1901 showed that 507 males were employed by the railway and in 1910 a Midland Railway Football Club was playing alongside the rail line at Engine Shed Lane. They are still playing today, although the name changed to Skipton LMS to mark the company's change of name.

The year 1911 saw a major national railway strike over wages and the Skipton men were joined by 1,500 textile workers who had struck a few days earlier and the two sets of workers expressed their solidarity at a mass meeting in Caroline Square. W Bellamy, the secretary of the Skipton branch of the Amalgamated Society of Railway Servants told the crowd that there were less than 12 men who had turned up for work but there was to be considerable disturbances over strike breakers. The Craven Herald reported that police had to escort the strike breakers to work but were followed by bands of union men who "in their excitement used language and threats that in their calmer moments they would probably regret". There were "turbulent" scenes outside the station and the police were called. Meanwhile the house of one railwayman who refused to join the strike, an RG Rankin, a magistrate, who lived in Keighley Road, was stoned and windows broken.

The disturbances worried the authorities, who feared that there would be even greater violence and 50 men were hurriedly sworn in as special constables. Their job was to carry out the duties of ordinary policemen, who were sent to supervise the scenes at the railway station and its approaches. The strike breakers spend at least one night in temporary accommodation at the station while pickets were set all round the area. A large crowd gathered at the station on the Saturday, August 19, but the large police presence calmed matters down. The strike was settled on the Sunday although it was Tuesday before all the men returned to work. A feature of the strike was the disruption it caused, not least to holiday makers who had been stranded and the mills, which were unable to obtain supplies or transport their finished goods.

A further strike occurred in 1919 but caused nowhere near as much disruption. The reason was the growing importance of road traffic - a sign of the threat to come to the future of the railways. In 1919 the Craven Herald reported heavy traffic on the roads as War Department lorries were pressed into service to move goods around and local bus companies were quick to exploit the gap. So much so that the General Strike of 1926 had little effect on the working of the district.

The decline of railway's power had set in and it was the Grassington line which was the first to go. It had always struggled to generate enough passenger traffic to be really profitable and there were complaints about the service. The growth of bus services marked its death knell and the last train ran on September 21 1930 when 54 passengers travelled to Skipton from Grassington. The line remained open to freight but was cut back to Swinden Quarry in 1969. Without the quarry the line would surely have been taken up but it provided a lifeline and in the early 1990s agreements were reached with the national park to promote more freight on to the line. As stated earlier, there are currently plans to introduce more passengers, tourist based, on to the new line to a new platform at Swinden.

The Midland Railway Company (which in 1923 had become the LMS – London, Midland and Scottish Railway) had, as we have seen, its doubts about the viability of the Ilkley to Skipton service from the start and there were rumours about its survival at the time the Grassington line was axed. However, it survived until the railway closure mania of the late 1950s and early 1960s and this line bit the dust in March 1965. At the same time, the only stations to remain open on the routes to Leeds and Bradford stations were at Keighley,

Bingley and Shipley. In January 1966 the line between Morecambe, Lancaster and Wennington closed, requiring trains from Skipton and the West Riding to the coast to divert via Carnforth. Three months earlier a branch line linking Barnoldswick with Earby had closed and in February 1970 the Skipton to Colne line route via Barnoldswick also shut.

Skipton station had become a sad sight. The attractive iron and glass awnings on the station were cut back, buildings on the island platform were demolished and the whole atmosphere was one of neglect and rot. The large engine shed closed (it is now a council depot) and the extensive sidings off Broughton Road were either lifted or became overgrown.

The future looked bleak for Skipton's railway but it held on by the skin of its teeth. A landmark date was the reorganisation of local government in 1974 when the West Yorkshire Passenger Transport Executive was formed to take control of bus and rail travel in the West Riding metropolitan area. Although Skipton lies outside the metropolitan area, in rural North Yorkshire, it was, however, seen as a natural commuter town for Leeds and Bradford, Due it coming under the control of North Yorkshire County Council rather than the two metropolitan authorities, fares to and from Skipton have never benefitted from the subsidised rates of the metropolitan districts, but without the WYPTE' s investment in the metropolitan part of the line, it is reasonable to assume that Skipton would have fallen by the wayside.

Between 1982 and 1990 stations were reopened. Cononley, for example, reopened in 1988 and there is currently agitation to reopen the Kildwick crossing station to service the growing community of Cross Hills. In 1995 the route was electrified and further timetable enhancements introduced. Improvements were made to the track and the station's canopies and awnings were restored to their former glory. Today the station is bustling again and the car park has had to be extended to cope with the growing numbers who see rail as the most efficient way to travel to Leeds, Bradford and beyond. Northwards the Settle to Carlisle line has also seen improvements with stations en route refurbished and the Ribblehead Viaduct restored and standing proud as a monument to the golden age of railway construction. The line is also being increasingly used for freight and with it there are increasing complaints about late night shunting noises along Broughton Road.

10: Riots

The route now takes us down a narrow path, signposted for Skipton Town Centre.

This path is known as Black Walk – due to the fact that old railway sleepers, black with oil and coal from the locomotives, were once used to line the walls. It crosses over Eller Beck, on its way from the castle to the river Aire. Around here there is a good view of Dewhurst's Mill and we are close by the site of one of the most sensational events in Skipton's history – the plug drawing riots of 1842.

The introduction of new power loom machinery around the mid 19th century was a source of great alarm for the labouring classes of Skipton.

They argued that the new machinery reduced the number of workers, thus lessening the earning capabilities of the family unit. In 1842 these fears led to the start in Lancashire of "The Plug Drawing Riots", so called because the agitators would pull the plug from the bottom of boilers, let out the water and extinguish the fire of the power looms. But the rioters also had another agenda: they were desperately hungry for food and the riots were often as much about looting to feed families. When they entered a town, businesses closed and windows were boarded up.

Writing in 1902, Dawson records the memories of one old Skiptonian who remembered the events of August 16 1842. She and her sister were playing near

Belmont Bridge when they saw a large body of men and women, four abreast, marching up Broughton Road towards Dewhurst's Mill and armed with sticks. The news spread like wildfire through the town. Magistrate Hastings Ingham went out to meet them and tried to persuade them to turn back, to no avail. While he rode to Burnley to fetch assistance, his fellow magistrates set themselves to swearing in special constables (there being just one parish constable, Thomas Ingham).

Dawson puts the number of rioters at 3,000 and they went to the mills owned by Mr John Sidgwick at Low Mills, Chapel Hill and High Mills in Skipton Woods and Dewhurst's Mill on Broughton Road where they pulled out the boiler plugs and halted the mills. Money was demanded of Sidgwick in return that the mob withdrew and, according to Dawson, was handed over. The mob did retreat, threatening to return if the mill was worked again without their consent. Meanwhile others went round the town, demanding money and carrying away food from looted shops and houses. The violence led to the magistrates reading the Riot Act in the market place before the rioters withdrew to a field known as Annahills, at the side of the road to Carleton, somewhere near where today the railway line passes the two supermarkets of Tesco and Morrison's.

Shortly afterwards the military, under the command of a Captain Jones, arrived, surrounded the mob and read the Riot Act again. Dawson wrote: "There is little doubt that the mob would have been quietly dispersed but for one of their number flinging a stone, which so severely injured a soldier that he died a few days afterwards. Mr Garforth, one of the magistrates, had one of his eyes so seriously cut by a stone flung at random that he lost the sight of the eye. Then the soldiers charged the mob with bayonets, driving them into a neighbouring lane, when they took to their heels, climbing over fence and hedge and falling into many a ditch but dispersing in all directions. Although no shot was fired and comparatively little blood was shed, this struggle has always since been known as the Annahills Fight".

Dawson, writing in 1902, was able to get eyewitness accounts lost to us today. He reports that a man with one leg got his wooden stump caught in the mud as he tried to cross a ditch. Soldiers, laughing, came to his rescue, leaving the wooden stump embedded in the mud.

A newspaper report 11 days after the riot: "This town has remained perfectly tranquil since the outrage of Tuesday the 16th, immediately after which the magistrates present, consisting of M Wilson, M Wilson jun, T Hastings Ingham and C Preston Esqrs., had a conference with the mill owners and pledged themselves to protect them by the presence of the military if they would immediately commence running their mills. This was instantly acted upon and we believe every workman in the town returned to his work. Some of the above magistrates have remained in the town day and night during the last week. In consequence of the disturbed state of Colne, Captain Jones of the 61st regiment was ordered back to that town and thus Skipton was left without military protection. The magistrates being determined to keep the mills running applied to Major-General Brotherton for troops and we are glad to say that a company of the 73rd regiment under the command of a Captain Widdington marched into the town and took control of the most comfortable barracks in the fine old castle of the Earl of Thanet. An example of energy has been shown by the magistrates and inhabitants of Skipton which, if it had been acted upon in other places, we are sure the course of these mischievous people would have been sooner checked. Measures are still in progress which it is hoped will ere long lead to the apprehension of more of the ringleaders in these riotous proceedings."

Six men were indeed apprehended – William Smith, 46, who appears to have been the ringleader, John Spencer, 50, William Spencer, 47, John Harland, 38, Edward Hey, 32, and James Dakin, 27. They were taken first to the Devonshire Hotel where the magistrates wasted no time in committing them for trial to York Assizes for "having at Skipton with force of arms, together with divers other evil-disposed persons riotously and tumultuously assembled to the terror of the Queen's subjects".

The trial took place in the September and two, Harland and Hey, were discharged when no evidence was offered against them. William Smith's counsel argued that he had led a starving mob in a creditable manner and his actions had in fact avoided bloodshed. There had been no injury to any persons (overlooking the blinding of magistrate Garforth's one eye) or property, save removing the water from the boilers. Needless to say, the judge, Justice Maul, was hardly impressed, directing the jury "If the practice was to be permitted of stopping mills until the delegation at Manchester permitted work to be resumed there would be an end to any government." He continued: "Any person who had joined the mob by whom these illegal acts were perpetrated, although they might not be proved to have taken an active part, still by their presence they rendered themselves responsible to the law."

The Chartist supporting newspaper the Northern Star reported Justice Maul as saying the court "was deeply indebted to the Government for the leniency they had shown in not prosecuting them for high treason or in having indicted them for robbery as was the case during the celebrated riots in London when a poor man asked for relief and got half a crown, for which he was afterwards hung on a charge of robbery".

The verdict was guilty; the jury believing the two Spencers were less culpable than the others. Smith was sentenced to 12 months' imprisonment with hard labour and the other three to six months hard labour.

Four days later six constables were sent to Barnoldswick to arrest John Greenwood (34) and John Hodgson (35) and a preliminary hearing at the Town Hall in Skipton heard that they had taken an active part in extorting money before committing them to trial. They were to stay in York prison until March 1843 when, with Hartley Stansfield (25) they came before the judge. Stansfield had secured bail on charges of rioting and assaulting JB Garforth. Stansfield denied assaulting the magistrate but did admit to hitting someone with a stick, for which he was sentenced to four months imprisonment with hard labour. The Barnoldswick pair, who had already been locked up for more than six months, were sentenced to a further month behind bars with hard labour.

As a footnote to this momentous day in Skipton's history, 30 or 40 young men of Skipton soon after banded together and headed for Linton and Grassington where they terrorised the locals and were handed bread, beer and in some cases money for them to go away. However, other farmers greeted them with loaded guns and the Skiptonians quickly turned heel. The riot quickly turned into a glorified pub crawl as they entered licensed promises and obtained ale on the threat that a much larger band was on its way from Skipton. News of the affair soon reached Skipton and a handful of special constables set off in pursuit. They were spotted approaching and the "rioters" fled in all directions. It is not recorded if any were caught.

Black Walk eventually spills out near the entrance to the Tesco supermarket and we are near the site of the town's first railway station

It would be remiss to ignore the Skipton Little Theatre, a little to the left on Cavendish Street. In 1960 the Skipton Players bought this old coach house which had stabling for three horses complete with mangers and a cobbled floor for £250. Mary Wales designed the Little Theatre and converted this coach house and stables into the Little Theatre at a cost of £2,000. It is one of the smallest theatres in the country whose auditorium has a capacity of just 78. The stage, measuring just 18 feet by 12 feet six inches, was built on the site of a loose box for horses. The first performance was The Mayor of Torontal in May 1960. Key members of the Skipton Players included Arthur Petherbridge, Norman Coy, Philip and Barbara Hurst, Charlie and Tony Rushforth. John Scott created many of the sets and Reg Waterhouse, reporter on the Craven Herald, wrote many of the reviews. In its report of the opening, the Craven Herald commented: "True, the Little Theatre with advantage have been a bit bigger. But it could not have been made larger without a lot of expensive new building work. The salient fact is that the theatre will be commodious enough for nearly all purposes the Skipton Players have in mind. The enterprise has already aroused widespread interest."

Before the opening of the Little Theatre the Skipton Players had performed in Skipton Town Hall and in Millfield Parish Church Rooms between 1934 and 1960.

The route now takes us down Carleton Street, between the Railway pub and the Craven Hotel (built to cater for trade from the new railway) towards Christ Church.

Christ Church was built in 1837 when the growing town population meant that Holy Trinity could not cope with the numbers. Christopher Sidgwick, of the mill owning family, compiled a Journal Book for Christ Church and he noted that while there were some 5,000 inhabitants of the parish, there was room for just 900 in the pews, plus room for about 250 children on benches and steps. So it was decided that another church was needed in the town, and it is interesting to note that Sidgwick records that of the 630 spaces envisaged, 270 were to be let or sold for an income to the vicar.

The Earl of Thanet was to give the land and the burial ground worth £500 to the new church and Sidgwick himself chipped in £500 with Christ Church, Oxford, providing land and buildings in the town, worth £1,000, as an endowment. Other donations amounted to £2,623.

The foundation stone was laid on June 21 1837 - the first time such a ceremony had been held in Craven for three centuries. Interestingly at the ceremony God Save the King was sung but in fact William IV had died the previous day but as the news had not reached Skipton the words God Save the Queen were not sung in honour of the Victoria. Building work continued until December, when the part built church was covered over. From March to November in 1838 the work continued and was nearly completed with the roof put on and doors and windows inserted, although the steeple was not finished. However, a violent storm in January 1839 blew in the west windows and damaged the roof. Nonetheless, the building completed by March and ready for consecration, carried out by the bishop of Ripon, on September 25 1839. The entire cost was £6,260 and completion required the formal division of Skipton into two separate parishes. Christ Church in Oxford, which as we have already seen had given land and buildings worth £1,000 in endowments, provided additional property in the town, including the tithe barn in Swadford Street, worth an extra £1,000.

The new church was gradually established to become a major force in the town. Indeed, as the town expanded, it was not long before Christ Church had far more inhabitants than the mother church, Holy Trinity. The growing congregation, led no doubt by the redoubtable Sidgwicks, wasted no time in developing the church. For example, in 1844 the six side windows were replaced by coloured glass and an east window of stained glass was inserted at a cost of £125. Ten years later three stained glass windows were placed at the west end of the church. The first vicarage was built in 1845 on part of the old tithe barn site donated by Christ Church, Oxford, on Ship Corner. The present vicarage is situated in Carleton Road on the fringes of the town and was built in 1900. Also in 1845 a school was built, Croft School, on Back Belmont Bridge next to Union Square to accommodate 140 children but it had to be enlarged in 1876 to take 167. This site was not very conducive to education. Union Square was the rough part of town and the road was described as a mud heap in dry weather, a swamp in wet with a dunghill, piggeries, privies, stables and manure all round. The present Christ Church School, opposite Tesco's in Craven Street, was built in 1893. Curiously, Dawson, writing in the 1940s commented; "The school has been scheduled for closure owing to site difficulties and its fate remains to be seen". It is still going strong 60 years later.

Gas was installed in 1873, allowing the first evening service to take place that year, an organ was added in 1905 and electric light came in 1925 and in

1946 a new east window was added. A church hall in Lower Union Street was built in 1936 at a cost of £2,500 and in 1939 the church had big plans to celebrate its centenary but these were thwarted by the outbreak of war.

The graveyard ceased to be used around the turn of the century but the inscription on one gravestone at the east end of the ground against the walls of the church is of especial note: "In memory of Edwin Calvert, son of Richard Calvert of Skipton, known by the title of the commander-in-chief. He was the smallest and most perfect human being in the world, being under 36 inches in height and weighing 25lb. He died in August 1859, aged 17 years."

As the road bends to the left, the walk continues straight forward down Gas Street, towards Gallows Bridge but, as a point of interest, it is worth a look to the right, towards the Keighley Road.

Eastwood's fish and chip shop has been administering its fish and chips to Skiptonians since before the war. It used to be adjacent to Robert Fell's lead works which were established in 1835 by John Fell and Forster Horner as a lead works, using lead extracted from the extensive workings in the Yorkshire Dales, particularly around Grassington and Hebden. There is a record of Robert Fell, who kept the Thanet's Arms pub in the town, also being a lead merchant although not a manufacturer. By 1881 Robert Fell and Sons was established, making sheet lead, water pipes and gas tubing. Later, as the local lead mining business declined and ceased as foreign imports flooded the market, the business developed into bathroom and plumbing works but closed in 1998 and in 1999 much of the building was knocked down for housing, although parts of the works were incorporated into the design. The front houses are to be named Tufton Place, after the family which owned the castle.

Next to Christ Church (to the right, viewing from this point of the walk) is one of the finest buildings in Skipton, Clifford House, now occupied by the solicitors JP Mewies and Co. This house was probably built for a wine merchant in the late 19th century but from 1901 was a doctor's surgery, the practice of Dr Waugh. Dr Norman McLeod joined in 1909 and was in practice until about 1938. His son, Iain McLeod, was born here on November 31 1910 and went on to become Chancellor of the Exchequer under Edward Heath's government. He was a great intellectual and of huge influence as a policy maker in the Conservative Party. However, on July 20 1970 he was found dead at 11

Downing Street from a heart attack. He is buried in the graveyard of St Andrew's Church, Gargrave.

Several independent general practitioners, including Dr McLeod were operating from Clifford House until 1938 when Cedric Robinson moved from Newmarket Street and amalgamated all the independents into one practice. Clifford House continued until 1982 when the partnership moved into the newly built Dyneley House Surgery on Newmarket Street.

Back to the walk, and we proceed straight ahead past the old Varley's foundry and it was the family's proud boast that their name was trodden upon by all Skiptonians. They refer to the grates and manhole covers around the town and, should you look down, there is a better than even chance that the name Varley will stare back at you.

The walk continues straight ahead to Gallows Bridge and over the canal footbridge back into the heart of the town.

11: Caroline Square

Having crossed Gallows Bridge, follow the footpath alongside Sunwin House, owned by the Yorkshire Co-operative to the pedestrian crossing and cross the busy Keighley Road, the main road south from Skipton.

Behind the Keighley Road shop fronts is the old working class area of Skipton known as Middletown, built at the time of the railway expansion. While the walk takes us to the left, once across Keighley Road, it may be worth a short detour to the right for some interesting buildings from the turn of the century.

First is the Unicorn Hotel, which originally was a small, two storey building attached to a row of cottages but knocked down in 1923 to make way for the current building. Next is the old Regal Cinema, once Skipton's grandest which showed all the best films, and now a nightclub, the After Dark.

The large building on the corner by the hump back bridge (currently housing a kebab takeaway on the ground floor) was the former Liberal Club, now known as Craven Hall. Opened on May 7 1898 it comprised a large assembly room on the first floor, snooker room, lecture and smoking rooms. The first floor windows on the corner open out on to a balcony from where political speeches were made. It served as a meeting point for the working class of the town and a photograph of 1910 shows a large gathering of railway workers outside the Liberal Club celebrating the end of a strike. It ceased to function as a Liberal Club during the

Second World War and afterwards passed into private hands. Many a Skipton child has learned ballet steps in Mrs Jaffe's classes held herein.

A little way round the corner, on Sackville Street itself, is the Temperance Hall, now the Plaza Cinema. The temperance movement was very strong in Victorian England and all across the country branches were set up to promote education in sober surroundings. The Skipton branch was started in 1838 and organised excursions and lectures and gradually found it needed a large base for its operations. It had many devotees, particularly among the town's affluent middle class and a foundation stone was laid on Whit Monday 1872 by Lady Frederick Cavendish and the Hall was opened on the Whit Monday of the following year at a cost of £1,200. The Temperance Hall had a large room for concerts, dances and meetings and also provided bed and breakfast type accommodation.

The 20th century saw the decline of the Temperance Movement and it is perhaps symbolic of the more hedonistic times that the foundation stone of the Temperance Hall was cut in half when the building was converted into the cinema by Mark Morris in 1912. The foundation stone, or at least the surviving half of it, can still be seen on the left hand side of the cinema. In about 1920 Matthew Hartley and Sons took over the cinema and later his son and daughter in law, Harry and Olive and then grandson Boris were to run the Plaza, meaning that three generations had brought films to Skipton for almost 80 years. In 1998 it passed out of the Hartley hands when it was taken over by Charles Morris, who still runs it as an independent concern. The Plaza has always been a one screen cinema and behind its plasterboard walls are the original ornate decorations, awaiting the call to be restored to their former glory.

One other cinema existed in Skipton, the Premier, which is now swallowed up by the Co-op's department store, called Sunwin House. This was situated over the Waller Hill Beck and was known as the "Rat Pit" and for good reasons as old Skiptonians tell dark tales of a customer being bitten by a rat during one screening. To hush the scandal up, the victim and his family were given free admittance for life. It closed in the 1950s and was incorporated into the Co-op store before demolition as part of the Sunwin House development in 1979.

After crossing Keighley Road at the pedestrian lights, we turn to the left and on to Caroline Square, a notorious bottleneck as four major roads converge at a roundabout and pedestrians take their lives in their hands as they attempt to cross the road. Hard to believe, but this was also Skipton's unofficial bus station. It is a busy spot, but an important point and worth pausing a while to take in the many points of note (we suggest stepping back a bit, alongside the Craven Pharmacy).

The very name Caroline Square harks back to a royal scandal from the late 18th century. The Prince Regent, later King George IV was perhaps the most indulgent of English monarchs, leading a life dedicated to pleasure. He was the son of George III, whose reign was interrupted by bouts of insanity causing the Prince of Wales to assume the role of monarch as Regent (hence the Regency Period. The story is memorably captured by the award winning film The Madness of King George). In affairs of the heart, the Prince was notoriously self indulgent and in 1784 he attempted to take Maria Fitzherbert, a well-born Roman Catholic widow as his mistress. She at first turned him down but when the Prince proposed a secret marriage she could not resist. They were married in the drawing room of her Mayfair house in December 1785. The marriage was reckless. While canonical, and thus in the eyes of the Church of England acceptable, it was also illegal under English law in two ways. By the Act of Settlement of 1701 marriage to a Catholic disqualified him and any children from succession to the throne and by the Royal Marriages Act of 1772 the absence of the sovereign's consent rendered the union invalid.

After nine years of unfaithfulness, the Prince Regent dumped Mrs Fitzherbert in order to make a bigamous marriage with a Protestant first cousin, Caroline of Brunswick, the Caroline of our story. The marriage was one of convenience; King George III, aware of the scandalous marriage to Mrs Fitzherbert, pressured his son into making a more appropriate match and one which ignored the unlawful one. The crucial factor was an agreement to pay a large part of the Prince's debts of £650,000, little less than an astounding £40 million in today's terms. Forced into marriage, the Prince took it out on his new bride and shunned her, much to the disgust of his future subjects, who took her side against an unpopular monarch. Perhaps the future George IV had cause to take exception to this forced, arranged marriage. Princess Caroline was no Princess Diana. Notoriously plain, even ugly, her personal hygiene was notoriously bad and she could match the Prince in her dissolute ways. She was far from a virgin and the Prince could bring himself to sleep with her no more than three times before banishing her to a life of scandalous immorality in Italy. Even so, the Prince's treatment of his bride caused outrage and mob riots. He put her on trial for adultery, excluded her from his 1821 Coronation (she turned up and was forcibly prevented from entering Westminster Abbey) and tried to have her name omitted from the church Litany in which the populace were asked to pray for her.

George influenced the Prime Minister, Lord Liverpool; a "Bill of Pains and Penalties against her Majesty" was introduced to divorce her, and Italian servants were brought into testify to her scandalous behaviour. The Bill was dropped by the Government and the country rejoiced at the King's discomfiture. The Leeds Mercury of November 18 1820 reported how a bonfire was lit in Skipton and effigies of her servants who had given evidence against her were burnt. She died suddenly in 1821 and the people of Skipton reputedly named the Square in her honour. However, the Mercury of 1820 refers to the effigies being burnt in Caroline Street, clearly suggesting that it was already known by her name. Whatever the origins, the name of an unpleasant woman is commemorated for evermore in Skipton because she was married to perhaps an even more unpleasant man!

The corner of Caroline Square, which bends away sharply down Keighley Road, is narrow, but once was much narrower still, a mere 23 feet wide. It was known as Ship Corner (the building on the corner opposite, where Sheep Street meets Swadford Street was the Ship Inn, which closed in 1924 and the Co-operative Insurance Society took over). It was a notorious bottleneck even in the days of horse and cattle drawn traffic and the Local Board of Health, which ran the town and was later to become Skipton Urban Council, obtained powers to borrow and spend £5,000 in removing obstructions and widening the corner to 42 feet.

Skipton's Post Office was situated in Swadford Street, further down from the Ship Inn. Skipton's early postal duties were a part time position. Dawson refers to a time in the mid 19th century when Skipton's postmaster was a "respectable aged dame" who discharged her duties from a modest office which was in part her dwelling house. She was succeeded by Robert Tasker, founder of the Craven Herald, who ceased to run his newspaper at 38 High Street upon taking up the position but still ran his printing and bookselling business from the premises. However, Tasker was not long in the post for in 1861 a John Faraday, also a tradesman, was in charge of running Skipton's post for five more years, from an unknown location but in 1866 the office of postmaster became a full time duty based in Sheep Street. In 1875 the office was removed to Caroline Square briefly before moving in to spacious premises in Swadford Street now occupied by a greetings card shop. Telegrams were first despatched and received in Skipton on New Year's Day 1870 and in 1888 the public telephone was introduced to the town. The current Post Office is housed inside the Co-op's Sunwin House.

Opposite the old post office and the former Ship Inn are Central Buildings. These were originally built in 1846 as the parsonage for the new Christ Church. However, in 1901 a new vicarage was built off Brooklands Terrace (now Carleton Court Residential Home for the elderly) and the premises were converted into a wine and spirit merchant's shop. Chew's Bar, also built in 1901 was named after Fred and Doris Chew, who ran the pub before the Second World War (they were later to run Overdale Country Club, on the Knaresborough Road) and finished at the Tennants Arms, Kilnsey. Swadford Street used to be a quiet thoroughfare of family residences but by 1900 it was becoming increasingly the shopping street it is today. The Cock and Bottle pub dates back to 1755 and on the corner of Coach Street, opposite Bizzie Lizzie's fish shop and now occupied by A Taste of Italy was the famous shop of Baldisoro Porri. Still viewing from this busy spot at Caroline Square is the hump-backed Belmont Bridge over the canal and, at its side Winterwell House now occupied by a sports shop. This was built in 1889 by John Varley and during its construction the old foundations of an old, large hall, were discovered. This was almost certainly Winterwell Hall, home of the Lamberts in the reign of Henry VIII. This was evidently a grand house named after a well which never froze in winter. The Lamberts, rich from rents, moved to Calton and John Lambert was to become a reliable general for the Parliamentarian cause in the next century. The last known date for occupation of the Hall was by Agnes Sawley in 1665 and the old house, or rather perhaps it ruins, were largely destroyed when the canal cut through its grounds.

Continuing our walk round Caroline Square, a plaque (ironically on the Woolworth's building) marks the site of the birthplace of Thomas Spencer, co-founder of Marks and Spencer. He was born the son of a shoemaker in 1851 in Queen's Court, which led off from the side of Woolworth's. He moved to Leeds to take up a job as book-keeper to the firm of Isaac Dewhirst. In 1894 Michael Marks and Israel Sieff asked Isaac Dewhirst to help set up their new company on Leeds market. Dewhirst declined but his book-keeper, who must have had independent means, stepped into the breach with a cash investment of £300 with Marks putting up £450. In 1904 Marks and Spencer opened their first store in Leeds centre. Thomas Spencer died the following year.

The square was also the site in the 19th century of travelling fairs which visited the town and it appears a scene was caused in 1877 when one poor resident was seized by a menagerie elephant. The creature had been taking titbits from the crowd when a shopkeeper on Brewery Lane was pushed forward a little and was seized by the elephant, who lifted him in the air, holding him aloft for sometime. Another incident occurred when the local people were awoken to a fearful din and found that one hyena had got loose into the cage of another and the two were locked in a fight. The keeper jumped in and started pummelling both animals with a club. One sneaked away but the other grabbed the keeper by the leg. He was quick thinking enough to bring the club down on its snout and it backed off with a scream, leaving the man with nothing worse than trousers ripped to shreds. Not surprisingly, the authorities took a dim view of these travelling circuses and in 1880 the surveyor to the Skipton Local Board of Health, William Bradley, ordered Jane Day, to take down her caravans as the board had no wish to see the streets blocked by cages of wild beasts. The redoubtable Mrs Day stood firm and the police were called, whereupon she threatened to turn her lions loose on them. The Craven Herald reported: "No Daniel among the police or the Local Board was courageous enough to try conclusions with the leonine species" and Mrs Day's show went ahead.

Victory for the circuses was only temporary, for in 1886 James Edmonds arrived with the 20 vans in his Wombwell's Menagerie and parked in Caroline Square for two days, for which he was served with 20 summonses. Despite appearing before the bench with a petition from shopkeepers in the near vicinity for him to be allowed to continue (doubtless there were spin-offs for them from the attraction), the magistrates showed the power of the authorities and handed out stiff fines. Chairman Hastings Ingham (the same magistrate who I have already described negotiating with the Plug Drawing Rioters) commented acidly that perhaps the shopkeepers would like to pay Mr Edmonds' fines for him.

Before the building of the bus station in 1950, Caroline Square served as an unofficial bus station, difficult though it is to imagine in these days when traffic is a severe problem at this bottleneck. Services run by West Yorkshire, Ribble, Pennine, Ezra Laycock and Silver Star services used the square as a dropping off point.

12: Newmarket Street

Passing Woolworths the walk takes us out of Caroline Square into Newmarket Street

BEFORE the Second World War Newmarket Street had become a rather squalid part of the town, with small cramped houses and insanitary conditions. While modern Skipton is thought of a highly desirable place to live, with property prices well above the average for the north, it is still essentially a northern mill town. It is worth quoting from an article in the Craven Herald to mark the Silver Jubilee of George V in 1935 and written by Arthur Smith, a director of Skipton Building Society.

Mr Smith refers to an unnamed Ermysted's headmaster just before the First World War describing Skipton as "consisting of serried blocks of dwellings, dreary and uninteresting". He complained that Skipton was full of cramped, inadequate housing with 60 houses per acre common, yet housing was in short supply. Up to the First World War whole streets were owned by one or two individuals. But the 1915 Rent and Mortgage Interest Restrictions Act changed the nature of housing in the town. Firstly the act prevented an increase in rent and secondly owners had to face a big increase in the cost of repairs. Immediately a house became vacant, property owners were quick to seize the opportunity to sell and invest the proceeds in securities giving a higher return. Other owners attracted by investments, gave tenants the opportunity to buy their homes often at a reasonable price. "In dozens of cases in our town advantage was taken of this offer, to the financial advantage of the buyer," said Mr Smith as a new post-war trend was born – buying for sale rather than buying for letting.

In its attempts to build "homes fit for heroes" returning from the trenches, the Ministry of Housing decreed that density should be no more than 12 an acre. Mr Smith wrote: "we find estates being built up giving to each house a nice plot of garden and other amenities and it is now no longer necessary for the housewife to spend her days in a drab, barren-looking building". In the pre-war years it was not considered necessary to provide a workman's house with a bathroom but in the 1930s it was a rare occurrence to build a house without a bathroom as the homes on the Regent's estate in Skipton proved. Yet there was also a decline in the number of bigger family houses – ones with attics and cellars. "These are a very difficult proposition when placed on the market and in the case of this class of property it is very difficult to obtain at least the pre-war price, " wrote Mr Smith. Yet today these big, terraced homes, usually on the west side of town, are very popular.

In 1927 the Daily Chronicle described Skipton's housing under the headline "The Worst Slums in the World", a description which outraged the chairman of Skipton Urban District Council, a Coun W Bellamy, who said that "no question has roused the resentment of the Skipton people more than this particular article". He continued: "There are few towns of the same age as Skipton that have fewer slum areas. The effort of this council for years past has been to try to deal with dwelling and areas that did not come up to present day standards. Nevertheless we have to remember that the present generation and many generations before are not responsible for the narrow alleys that exist."

Newmarket Street was to benefit from the slum clearances, although the replacement buildings further down are far from architecturally pleasing.

At the High Street end, most of the older buildings survived the slum clearance. John Phillip, TV and electrical goods' shop at 28 Newmarket Street, was built by John Carr and later became the residence of general practitioners, the last of whom, Cedric Robinson, moved to Dyneley House in 1938. In 1956 Dr Robinson sold this house to John Phillip for his radio and TV business, which had started as electrical engineers and contractors in 1926 operating from a building (now demolished) in Black Walk. In 1929 John Phillip merged with the Craven Motor Company in High Street, Skipton, and began selling radios and gramophone records. The business moved to Sackville Street (in 1938) and then to Otley Street (in 1949) before its move to its current address.

A large Government building set just off the main street hosts the Social Security offices and replaced a former bus garage operated by the West Riding Road Car Company. It is an unlovely building, large and lacking in character.

The Devonshire Hotel is second only to the Black Horse in terms of size and was built between 1790 and 1813 and was known as the New Inn until 1821. Richard Boyle, earl of Cork and Burlington, is believed to have been the architect and his daughter married the Duke of Devonshire, the change of name presumably reflecting this union. It provided accommodation for stage coach travellers and there was stabling at the rear for horses. Now a splendid bowling green is situated behind the pub. In March 1897 it was sold at auction for £6,050 to a Mr JH Lloyd of Colne but apparently the business declined, for in 1911 it was sold together with its 18 bedrooms, billiard room and bowling green for just £2,830 to Joshua Tetley's Brewery, Leeds at an auction held at the brewery itself.

On the opposite side of the road is Craven Books, a fine house which dates back to at least 1783, when records show that it was owned by Samuel Atkinson and John Dewhurst. In 1821 a Miss Wimberley was running a girls' school from there. By the 1870s it was known as The Armoury.

By Heseltine's newsagency we are about to turn right down a narrow alley called The Ginnel but it is worth mentioning two other buildings on Newmarket Street.

A little further along and on the same side as the newsagent's is Dyneley House Surgery, home to one of the two Skipton medical practices. Readers may remember the practice set up in Clifford House on Keighley Road. This moved to this new site in 1982, a purpose-built surgery with each doctor having a consulting suite. The facilities were later enlarged with the addition of a barn conversion and large nursing extension. The site dates back to 1748 when the large Dyneley House was built there. The Dyneleys and their descendants lived there until the mid 1800s when John Bonny Dewhurst was tenant from 1851 to 1866 (again readers may remember that he was to move to Aireville in 1869). Moving in after Dewhurst was a director of the Craven Bank, Col George Robinson, whose son, George Geoffrey Robinson, was to become editor of The Times. In 1911 William Carr moved into Dyneley House and established a

Temperance Hotel there, Dyneley Hotel. The house was to remain a Temperance Hotel until its closure in the mid 1960s and the land and building were derelict until knocked down to create the surgery.

Across the road is the large, imposing, concrete edifice that is the telephone exchange. This used to be a six bedroom private dwelling, Stanley House, which was knocked down as part of the general clearance of the 1950s to make way for the telephone exchange, opened in April 1954.

We turn down the Ginnel to head to the Quaker's Meeting Room.

The Quakers meeting room was founded in 1693 and the movement has a long history in Skipton. It is just possible that George Fox, founder of the sect of Friends, may have visited Skipton as early as 1652. Records speak of him "entering a market town on market day" after he had "left Bradford on his way to the Yorkshire Dales". He certainly visited Skipton in 1658 and the records show that this was a time of great hardship for his followers. Quakers were attacked and set upon for preaching, although the fate of William Simpson might have been less open to sympathy for Dawson, who also wrote a History of Nonconformism in Skipton, quotes records that he preached naked and was beaten up and cut with a knife

Rev Robert Sutton and his son, Thomas, both vicars of Skipton between 1621-1665 and 1665-1683 were particularly hostile in their attitude to Quakers. Oliver Heywood, a Nonconformist wandering preacher who was a frequent visitor to Skipton and surrounding villages in his diary of 1681 notes that the vicar, Thomas Sutton was found drunk in the company of others and became abusive. "He is a strange man, he will drink till 3 or 4 o'clock on Sabbath Day morning yet preach and rant it against drunkenness, notably in the pulpit." However, the parish register speaks of him as being "the best of preachers and a very peaceable good man". The persecution against Nonconformists and Puritans was brought to an end by the Toleration Act of 1689. Licenses were obtained for houses to become meeting places.

The walk continues down The Ginnel and opens into a play area.

Back in the 1970s this area was swampy, rutted and partly covered by the concrete base of an old Nissen hut but in 1977, to mark the Silver Jubilee of

Queen Elizabeth II, the Civic Society stepped in to clear and grass this area and put a low wall around it. The town council also stepped in and donated £1,500 towards the play area. A path also leads off to the right, after crossing the Waller Beck, and local scouts, Air Training Corps, Army Cadets and schools all became involved in improving this area. Aireville School's contribution was outstanding as they made a footbridge, kissing gates and seats. The whole project cost some £6,000, of which £2,500 came from a Queen's Jubilee Fund grant and £2,000 by appeal. Another £450 came from Dr Cedric Robinson, from his testimonial fund.

The Waller Beck here flows eastwards and eventually links up with Eller Beck, which flows into the town from the south. While tranquil and pleasant most times, in fact Waller Beck has been a source of some grief to Skipton over the years.

The town's situation at the base of the Rombalds Moor has made it prone to flooding and on four occasions in the 20th century there was considerable destruction in the town due to cloudbursts. Perhaps the worst came on June 3 1908 when a localised cloudburst centred on Rylstone Fell, just to the north of the town, caused a flood which destroyed a mill in Embsay and wrecked havoc in Skipton. Eller Beck smashed through Skipton Woods, taking with it bridges, trees and other debris and destroying the Round Dam. The beck normally runs alongside Springs Canal but some 12 feet below the canal bank. On this occasion it rose and merged with the canal, which was some six feet above its normal level. Skipton Brewery was engulfed, losing half its beer.

In 1968 another flood hit the town. The cottages at the base of Grassington Road were flooded and large hailstones the size of marbles covered the street.

The flood of June 13 1979 saw the death by drowning of one Skiptonian, Miss Jane Barraclough, who lived in a cottage in Brookside, off Newmarket Street. The 87-year-old's body was found in her house which was flooded to a depth of five feet. Three men, Robert Heseltine, Ian Barraclough and Mick Jaunzens, were commended by the coroner at the subsequent inquest for their efforts in coming to the rescue of many of the old people who lived in Petyt Grove and its vicinity. Again an unusually violent burst of rain had caused the flood which occurred around lunchtime. Heavy rain, which seemed to have been localised on the hilltops overlooking the town, swept down into the town and Waller Beck was unable to cope. The houses alongside were badly affected and at Dewhurst's the looms and electrical gear were completely underwater, halting production. When the authorities came to investigate the causes it was stated that a hot spell before the flood had caused a crust on the surface thus much water which might have soaked in instead ran off down the two becks, Wilderness and Jenny Gill, which meet at the top of Newmarket Street. To aggravate the situation debris washed down, blocking the culverts and causing the flood to back up around Petyt Grove. Later Yorkshire Water Authority was to say the floods were exacerbated by the amount of rubbish, particularly garden refuse, being tipped into the becks by householders. However, such a flood only happened once every 100 years, they reassured the townsfolk. Incidentally the mayor organised a flood relief fund which ran for six weeks and raised £15,846 in donations

Despite the "once in a 100 years" assurances, there was a repeat on June 11 1982 when more than an inch of rain was recorded in less than three hours in Skipton. However, even more was thought to have fallen on Rombalds Moor, and eyewitnesses spoke of three separate rivers heading down the steep hillside into the east of the town. It all collected in the Newmarket Street area, engulfing shops and again pensioners had to be rescued from their homes in Petyt Grove – this time without loss of life.

The Co-op's newly opened store, Sunwin House, was flooded to a depth of two feet and thousands of pounds worth of electrical goods and foodstuffs were destroyed. Other shops in the area also suffered and there was severe criticism of the council, which had written off the 1979 flood as a freak, for failing to clear blocked culverts which subject had been raised three years previously.

Proceed to the bridge over Waller Beck. Turn left after the bridge and along the footpath through the woods. Cross the bridge and into Petyt Grove.

The old people's bungalows on Petyt Grove are on the site of Tradesman's Place, Club Houses, Greenside and the Cross Keys pub, scene of some of the worst housing mentioned at the start of the chapter. The houses were built by the Tradesmen's Sick Club; a mutual self-help society but they became notorious as insanitary slums prone to flooding. The tightly packed houses were pulled down in 1958 and Petyt Grove, with its old people's bungalows and open expanses, built in its place in 1963. A large stone nameplate for Tradesman's Place can still be seen across the road on Newmarket Street.

On the opposite side of the road is the Church of St Andrew's. The first

Independent Chapel was built between 1777 and 1779 (before that a building on the site of the present Devonshire Hotel had been used). Rev Samuel Phillips of Keighley bought the plot of land on Newmarket Street for forty pounds and six shillings. A mortgage of £100 was then raised to complete the building of a chapel, which replaced a cottage. Adjoining land was later purchased for nine pounds and two shillings to serve as a burial ground. The congregation grew steadily and a new, larger building was planned to accommodate the extra numbers. In September 1838 the last worship was conducted in the original chapel and future services were to be held at the Hole in the Wall pub on the High Street until the new chapel was completed in July 1839 at a cost of £1,300. Mill owner John Dewhurst gave £115 for a new organ. Further extensions and improvements were made in 1863 (during which time the congregation moved to the more appropriate surroundings of the Town Hall). In 1877 there were yet more plans to expand (this was a period when the town's population was growing rapidly) but a trade depression called a halt to these plans and it never went ahead. Instead a building fund was established and its proceeds went towards building a new Sunday school which opened in 1890.

Arial: Mills, canal and railway - back to back

Above:
Ermysted's. Two top schools keep house prices high.

Left:
Brewery Lane

Broughton Road and Dewhurst's Mill

Skipton Little Theatre

Christchurch for a time outgrew Holy Trinity

Sheep Street from Caroline Square

The Society of Friends' Meeting House - The Ginnel

St Andrews Methodist and United Reform Church on Newmarket Street

Old Ermysted's Schoolroom, electrified

The Grotto in The Wilderness - a shrine to St James?

Autumn tranquillity in The Wilderness

Skipton Baptist Church - Otley Street

Craven Court, appreciated by Prince Charles

Skipton Millennium Walk - The End

13: Shortbank Road

The walk crosses Petyt Grove to Newmarket Street to take in St Andrews Methodist and United Reform Church and then turns right towards the roundabout Shortbank Road.

AT the foot of Brougham Street, on the right as the walk progresses, is the Park Shed, built by Thomas Wilkinson, the owner of a number of Lancashire mills, in 1889 and the first mill to be built away from the canal side. A more modern industry, Castle Acoustics, manufacturers of high quality speakers, currently conduct a highly successful business from here.

Crossing Brougham Street by the mill head for the Cross Keys, relocated from its original site off Newmarket Street and attached to the former grammar school.

This is the foot of Shortbank Road, which was the old road to Ilkley. Built by the Romans it was part of the route between the major centres of York and Ribchester and came over the tops of Skipton road with a steep descent down into the town. The poet Thomas Gray (of 'Elegy Written in a Country Churchyard fame') described Shode Bank, as it was then called, as "the steepest hill I ever saw a road carried over in England". The King's judges, as they went on circuit from York to Lancaster, were said to dread the descent down Shode Bank. Almost certainly because of the difficulty of the descent a new road from Addingham to Skipton via Draughton was built in 1803 but the old road is still a thoroughfare, providing spectacular views and the terrain encourages youngsters on motorbikes to practice their trial riding skills. Halfway down the hill is an old toll booth, built in the 18th century to collect the tolls of the travellers coming down the road.

This high moor above the town was the source of Skipton's water supply for many years. In 1823 a company was formed and a small reservoir was constructed on a site called Jenny Wharton's Gill and water carried to the town in iron pipes. So the townsfolk gradually ceased to use wells and streams with water of doubtful quality. But as the town grew in size, so the Jenny Gill reservoir ceased to be sufficient to meet the demand and the Local Board of Health took the problem into their own hands by buying up the private waterworks. They built a new and larger reservoir close by, drawing its supply from the Whinny Gill stream, at a cost of about £30,000. After a few years this source of water proved inadequate also and in October 1903 Skipton Urban Council decided upon the construction of a reservoir of 140 million gallon capacity below the moor at Embsay.

There was much debate about the location of this new reservoir. Some wag at the Craven Herald produced a pamphlet lampooning the characters entitled "The Pied Piper of Skipton."

Up at the top of the tarmaced section of this road were Skipton's old baths, as well as the source of her water supply. In 1833 a Dr Dodgson built the first Skipton public baths which were connected to a sulphur spring. Apparently Dr Dodgson had hopes of establishing Skipton as a spa town to rival Harrogate but his dreams turned to dust and he died in the workhouse in 1866 and these baths fell into disrepair.

In 1906 John Scott leased the old reservoir in Short Bank and converted it into baths and pleasure gardens. These baths consisted of an open air swimming bath, a covered swimming bath and ladies and gents slipper baths. On the open air pool there was also boating and fishing. These baths were the scene of Skipton swimming galas and diving competitions. A water polo team was housed here and photographs show large crowds in attendance. In 1959 these baths were closed to the public on health grounds and in 1964 the new pool at Aireville was opened.

Before crossing the bridge over the beck on Shortbank Road, turn left past an electricity sub-station.

The electricity sub-station is the site of Ermysted's Grammar School (see earlier chapters). A plaque above the entrance states "This 16th century building was originally the chapel of St James of the Knights Hospiteller of St John of Jerusalem. It subsequently passed into the hands of Canon Ermysted, who housed the Grammar School here which he provided in 1548". This building is not the 16th century original but has been rebuilt, probably in the 19th century, on the same site. The Urban District Council had bought the old grammar school building in 1899 and it was turned into an electricity sub-station in 1923. Electric lighting was the privilege of a few, wealthy folk before then and the supplies were all private. In 1922 the Urban Council entered the market as a purveyor of electricity obtained from the Western Electricity Company and in the following year they struck a deal with the Yorkshire Electric Power Company for supply in bulk, agreeing to use the old school building as a sub station. From this date both electric light and power could be obtained by private consumers on reasonable conditions. The Urban Council was not slow to extend its provision of power to nearby villages and by the end of the Second World War and privatisation, a further six sub stations had been brought into use. Gas was also provided by the Urban Council. In 1899 the council obtained an Act of Parliament empowering it to buy the plant and rights of the privately owned Skipton Gas Company, based in Cavendish Street.

To the side of the old Ermysted's School is a footbridge which lines up with an old bridleway which runs uphill to Wensleydale Avenue and the open fields. Cross the bridge and notice how the line of the bridge has been diverted from an earlier line that would have hit the newer bigger school hall. The entrance into The Wilderness is just a few metres along the on the left.

The Skipton Civic Society purchased this area for £500 from Whitbread Breweries in 1999. Their secretary, Gwynne Walters, has striven to raise the £28,000 needed to bring about the necessary improvements. The new bridge across Wilderness Beck and the new steps out onto Otley Street (due for completed in 2000) will reclaim this area from a glorified dog loo into an open amenity area serving the Shortbank and Regent's area of the town and part of the Millennium Walk.

After the floods of 1979 numerous cars washed down from Peter Clark Autos garage were recovered in this area, including some perched in the trees. One Ford car had been returned guarantee as it had been "letting in water". Peter Clark's garage later relocated to the Airedale Business Park and the land upstream, further east on Otley Road, was used for new housing in 1995.

On the banks of Wilderness Beck in the wood there is a strange structure. It is an age-distressed partially formed dome, lined in render, into which have been fixed an eight-rayed star of small scallop shells. The scallop shell is the symbol of St James. It is probable that this is a 16th or 17th century shrine to St James, perhaps the work of boys from Ermysted's. It may have been associated with the eight day market of St James that used to be a fixture in the calendar of Skipton. The structure was featured on 19th century maps but was noted as run down in the 1930s. Seventy years on it remains sadly neglected.

After a pleasant walk through the wood, a newly created set of steps (due to be completed in 2000) takes us up to Otley Road. Turn left past the Cross Keys pub (which moved to this site from Newmarket Street) and cross the road to the police station.

The police station was built in 1878 and first used in 1879. It is the headquarters of the Craven Division of North Yorkshire Police.

In 1953 the Soroptimist Club of Skipton raised money to convert derelict land at the corner of Otley Road and Newmarket Street into a garden and named it Coronation Garden, as it was opened in the year of the Coronation of Queen Elizabeth II. Seats were given by the Soroptimists and various other organisations.

The final leg of our Walk takes us back to the High Street via Otley Street, a relatively new part of the town. Otley Street opened in 1844 when an entrance was effected on the High Street. Originally called New Street, it led to Otley Road, the junction being by the police station as the alignment of the houses show.

14: Elementary schools

On the right as the walk proceeds down Otley Street is the former Parish Church School.

Two of Skipton's largest schools were based on Otley Street – the Parish Church School and the British School. The Parish Church School is now used by Craven College and a Youth Centre while further along Otley Street, tucked away behind the frontage, was the British School. The fortunes of some of Skipton's schools have been dealt with in varying depth in previous chapters; it now seems an opportune point to look at elementary education in the town.

A small school had been operating in the grounds of Holy Trinity from the mid-sixteenth century and operated by the parish clerk. It was in a state of decay at the beginning of the 19th century and in 1813 a meeting was called to discuss the situation. A committee was formed for the purpose of setting up a completely new school. The Earl of Thanet was approached and he agreed to hand over a piece of land in Rectory Lane (now the site of the Three Links Club) on which to site the new establishment. The site secured, a subscription list was opened which raised £305 and the school was erected and completed by 1814. It was one room and could accommodate 200 boys. The success of this venture persuaded the committee to seek to establish a school for girls and again the owner of the castle came up with the land, on the opposite side of the road in what is now a private house. The girls' school opened in 1816.

While the town had subscribed generously towards the financing of the two schools, they were constantly short of money. In 1832 the managers decided that the children would have to pay for their own books and in 1840 they appealed to the townsfolk for funds to pay for extra repairs.

There were a number of private schools in existence in the town, although their history is brief, details sometimes confined to advertisements or entries in almanacks. Among those we know of was one operated by a Benson Bailey in Water Street between at least 1830 and 1848. Sarah Cooper was operating another in High Street between 1837 and 1853. As we have seen Christopher Sidgwick also opened a school in Water Street to cater for children employed in his mills. It lasted only for four years.

The first master at the new Parish Church boys' school was James Hall, who had been in post at the clerk's school in the grounds of Holy Trinity. Despite re-appointing him, the school committee was often in conflict with the master. In 1834 they twice fined him for "irregularity" and in April 1835 they warned him that if he was found drunk in the next three months he would be dismissed. He lasted until 1838 when the committee records show that "in consequence of the drunkenness and irregularity of James Hall, continued in defiance of repeated warnings he has had, be dismissed from his office". Hall was to run, briefly, a private school in Newmarket Street.

He was succeeded by Christopher Sidgwick, who was clearly a man of independent means, being part of the mill owning family. A devout man, he was the same Christopher Sidgwick behind the financing of Christ Church. He did not last long at the Parish Church school, falling out with the committee when he argued that accommodation provided in Holy Trinity during the Sunday Service was so poor that the children could neither see nor hear and therefore they should attend Christ Church. When the committee refused he resigned and set up his Water Street establishment.

Meanwhile the first head of the girls Parish Church School, a Miss Grave, lasted but three years. Her successor, Ann Gudgeon, was to be in post for more than 30 years. She seems to have been well liked for, despite the tight finances, the committee financed an extension to the mistress's dwelling house (no house was provided for the boys' school master). She retired in 1851 when she was 78 years old.

The Parish Church schools were Anglican and run by a committee connected to Holy Trinity. However, Nonconformism was strong in Skipton not least in the form of the mill-owning Dewhurst family. In 1844 John Dewhurst provided a temporary classroom and in 1846 he opened at a personal cost of £350 a new school in between Newmarket and Otley Streets. This school earned a glowing early inspectors' report and soon outgrew its premises. The British Society, an organisation which funded non-denominational school construction, agreed to provide a grant providing the school was in the hands of a board of trustees and in August 1856 contracts were drawn up to expand the school. The British School became in effect, a Congregationalist School. John Dewhurst, who had been mainly responsible for the construction of the Congregational Chapel (now known to us as St Andrews) in 1839, was its main financer. Its committee of trustees was dominated by Congregational Church members. While the committee of the Parish Church were prominent businessmen drawn from what might term the top strata of the town's society, the managers of the British School were shoemakers, coal merchants, drapers and chandlers.

The Wesleyans in the town were also setting up their own school. It opened in Wesley Place, on Keighley Road, now occupied by the bus station, in January 1845. Like the British School, the committee was made up of small businessmen – no less than five shoemakers and four grocers served. From the start it proved popular and within 18 months the committee was planning to build an infants' classroom but their hopes were hindered by a lack of finance. The infants' classroom plan was abandoned in favour of a curtain to divide off part of the building. A solution to the problem came in 1865 when the new Wesleyan Chapel was built in Water Street in 1845. The old chapel, on Chapel Hill, became vacant and the Wesleyan community took the decision to utilise its space as a solution to the problems of their cramped school.

Also opening in 1845 was a school for the new parish of Christ Church. Funds were sought from the National Society, an organisation which, like the British Society, provided grants for building schools but, unlike the British Society, insisted that they follow strict Anglican teaching. The new parish of Christ Church catered for the massed terrace houses springing up as homes of the labourers in the burgeoning textile industry and it found great difficulty raising sufficient funds from the local community to finance the school. Still they managed to raise £210 towards the £365 required, with grants from the National Society bridging the gap so that the school opened on Back Belmont

Bridge with room for approximately 150 pupils. It was frequently referred to as the Croft School although for clarity I shall refer to it as Christ Church School.

Thus by the middle of the century the following elementary schools were open: Parish Church (Rectory Lane, opened 1814 (boys) and 1816 (girls), accommodation for 287), British School (Otley Street, opened 1845, accommodation for 328), Wesleyan (Wesley Place, Keighley Road, opened 1845, accommodation for 181), Christ Church (Belmont Bridge, opened 1845, accommodation for 132), St Stephen's R.C. (Gargrave Road opened 1854, accommodation for 314). It is worth noting that the 1844 Factory Act required young children employed in factories to attend school on a half day basis for five days a week. Three of these schools – British School, Christ Church and Wesleyan – opened the following year.

The schools were controlled not by authorities but by local committees, who had to raise the funds. One way was by subscriptions from attenders at the churches connected to these schools but an important source of revenue was payment from the pupils, known as school pence. For example, in 1853 the British School published a bill stating that it charged two pence a week for infants, three pence for juniors and four pence for seniors. Successive governments introduced and gradually increased the grants to schools.

The standard of education in these early schools often left much to be desired. Few teachers had any formal qualifications. Teaching was often in the hands of "pupil teachers" – apprentices drawn from the ranks of the students. Often they dropped out, either because the wages were so low or they were patently not up to the job, which also expected them to sweep the floors and clean the stoves. William Heap was the son of a master at the Parish Church School but attended Christ Church School. As a pupil teacher there he had many failings, the master noting in the log book that he made more spelling mistakes than his pupils and his knowledge of British rivers was inferior to that of a nine year old. Heap also encouraged children to bring him gifts of fruit, sweets and tobacco and he was reprimanded in front of the whole school. One parent withdrew his children from Christ Church because of Heap's bad language. Not surprisingly, in 1871, young Heap was sacked. At the British School one pupil teacher was sacked for theft. Not all were failures though and a number did go on to complete their apprenticeships and even become qualified.

The Education Act of 1870 ordained for the first time that a school should be within the reach of every child (compulsory attendance was introduced in

1880) and provided for the provision of School Boards, secular bodies which controlled education in a district. However, these were not compulsory and the five voluntary schools continued to control elementary education in the town. A major impact of this Act on Skipton schools was that building grants to voluntary schools were to cease after a 12 month period of grace. While some schools were struggling financially and could not hope to raise sufficient funds to add to the grants, the managers of Parish Church were aware that the schools on Rectory Lane were in a poor state. The Bishop of Ripon described them as "inconveniently placed, incommodious, decayed and dilapidated and unfit for the purpose for which they existed". The managers looked into an extension at the cost of £200 but decided that a new build, at a cost of £2,000 was the better solution. They raised £1,050 in subscriptions and, after a pledge from the government of £595 and £140 from the National Society, they pressed ahead. The new Parish Church School was opened in Otley Street in 1874 with room for 600 pupils but its cost had spiralled to £3,500. Appeals and fund raising events had to be held in the town and it was to be 1878 before the debt had been paid off. The Parish Church was to further expand in 1895 when it opened an Infants School at Millfields, Coach Street (the building which was later to become Coffee Care).

While one National School, Parish Church, was able to move into larger premises, the other, Christ Church, or the Croft School, had a longer wait. In 1873 the managers reported on the "enormous disadvantages arising from the situation of the school; proximity of the canal; the wharf where stones, timber and other heavy articles are usually lying; the blacksmith's forge at which a large number of horses are shod; Union Square and its inhabitants; again the damp and dirty road leading to the building – a mud heap in dry weather and a swamp in wet; then the dunghill, privies, piggeries, stables and manure tanks on all sides. Considering all this it was deemed folly to spend much on the present schoolroom and urgently necessary to make an effort to erect a new building on a better site." The wish did not become reality. Indeed classrooms were doubled in size, new windows installed and ceilings raised but the school was generally considered at the bottom of the system. By 1890 the population of the parish had trebled but the number of places available had barely risen, from 147 to 167.

It seems though that children were crowded in as turning away pupils was turning away revenue. Indeed, there was some unscrupulous book keeping to balance the books. Two registers were in operation, one for the master and the other for the inspectors showing a much lower figure. This came to an end when an inspector made an unannounced visit and the number of infants was strictly limited (infants, of course, paying less). To ease the situation a saleroom in Romille Street was rented at a cost of £20 a year.

In 1878 there was a serious attempt to move but the problems of financing Parish Church's move was enough to cause some doubts in the parish. On the other hand, the castle authorities were prepared to lease a plot of land at the top of Castle Street for use as a school and Christopher Sidgwick, the driving force behind the construction of Christ Church and its school, died in that year and it was considered to be a fitting memorial to him. The proposal was quietly dropped.

In 1885 a new school was again talked about with the Castle Street site still available but the objection this time was that the cost of carrying stone etc up the steep hill would add to the building costs. By 1890 though the situation was intolerable and the success of the Wesleyans in building a new school (see below) perhaps was taken as a challenge. Land was acquired on Craven Street and the new Christ Church School opened in September 1893. The master expressed relief at leaving "the prison-like Croft School". There was a hint of scandal however, publicised in the Craven Herald, as the vicar was accused of misappropriating £120 subscribed. The explanation was that it was used to support the temporary infants' room in Romille Street. That did not help efforts to raise subscriptions but the intervention of the Archbishop of Canterbury did help matters. Archbishop Benson was a cousin of Christopher Sidgwick and married to a daughter of William Sidgwick, a headmaster of Ermysted's Grammar School. His chaplain wrote to the National Society in support of an application of a large grant for a new Christ Church School: "He desires me to tell you," wrote the chaplain, "how very deserving the case to be. His Grace has known Skipton all his life and can testify to the poverty which exists in the parish of Christ Church and to the good work which has long been going on. Outside help is much needed and his Grace is sure that a grant from the National Society could not be better bestowed than for the purpose named." In 1895 the managers debated whether or not to rename Christ Church the Benson Memorial School.

The third school to move to a new site between the middle and turn of the century (Ermysted's of course being another) was the Wesleyan School.

Opened in 1845, we have seen how they moved to the former chapel in 1865. Inspectors were not happy with its echoing schoolrooms and the managers were worried about the proximity of the Corn Mill dam. In 1890 the foundation stone was laid for a new school behind the Wesleyan Chapel. In the same year they also opened a school for infants in the Christ Church Parish, Trinity Infants School

The schools found varying degrees of difficulty in financing their new buildings and running the schools, relying heavily on subscriptions and fund raising events. Schooling was now compulsory but the children were still expected to pay (an Act of 1891 had abolished school pence for younger ones and reduced the amount which could be charged for older ones). The Wesleyan School master reported in his register of 1883 that "the Cassons and Hardacres have been dismissed because they would not pay their weekly fees. Warnings plenty have been given but all have been received without attention being paid to them, so I resolved to act". Christ Church and Parish Church log books also show instances of some families finding it hard, if not impossible to pay the school pence, especially in times of unemployment. By 1900 the British School had a debt of £343 and wanted the County Council to take over the running of the school, Christ Church owed more than £650 and the Wesleyan School owed £427, prompting the treasurer to write: "so large has the debt now become that although government grants and receipts from the school pence are larger than ever they are not sufficient to place the school in a solvent position."

The 1902 Education Act was the saviour for these schools. Local School Boards were abolished (although of course none existed in Skipton) and their schools came under the control of the county council. More significantly for Skipton, schools could retain their "voluntary aided" status which meant they had to continue financing most of the costs relating to the fabric of the building. Thus Parish Church School continued with its money-raising activities (one large drive was to install electricity in the 1930s) as the West Riding County Council funded only a small portion of the costs. This was probably the main reason why the Parish Church School decided to change its status in 1950 to a "controlled" school. Managers of the voluntary schools, in return for providing the buildings, were to retain the appointment of teachers while their expenses were to be met out of the rates. What this in effect did was end the system in Skipton of subsidising schools from bazaars, jumble sales and subscriptions and put them "on the rates". School pence was abolished.

The changes of 1902 were bitterly opposed by Nonconformists nationally because they feared that Church of England would be taught during religious instruction but on a local level it at least saved the school at Water Street from collapse. It and Christ Church became controlled schools.

In 1909 the British School, having outgrown its premises, moved to a new building in Brougham Street and adopted the street as its new title, Brougham Street Council School. In 1958 the Parish Church School moved and merged with its old "rival" in the Brougham Street premises.

15: Otley Street

In 1939 a medical practice moved into the row of cottages next door to the Parish Church School. Four terraced houses were transformed into a surgery with four consulting rooms and a reception and dispensary. The doctors installed a petrol pump behind the surgery for their benefit. The Otley Street practice, which was established in 1939, was the first group practice of General Practitioners in this country as previously doctors had practised on an individual basis. It was the brainchild of Dr Guy Ollerenshaw. In 1995 the Otley Street Surgeries moved to its new premises off Coach Street, renamed The Fisher Medical Centre. The original building is now the home of Medacs, a highly successful business which finds medical placements. The eastern cornerstones are particularly interesting, with carvings

The Skipton Baptist Chapel at the corner of Otley Street and Rectory Lane was built in 1860 and the opening service took place in June 1861.

Two courts stand in Otley Street. The oldest by far is the county court, built in 1847. Over the doorway are the arms of Queen Victoria. Further along Otley Street is the magistrates' court, opened in May 1973. Opposite the courts is Armoury House, built in 1892, when the premises in Newmarket Street were vacated. It was here that the Skipton territorial army would meet. In the 1970s it became a billiard hall and was later converted into offices, housing renowned architects Bowman Riley.

The Albion pub was the first building to be constructed when this part of Otley Street was widened in the middle of the last century.

To the left, off Court Lane, lies Skipton Building Society's former headquarters. Before the war the site was the headquarters of Nicholas Smith's haulage business before their move to the outskirts of the town on Gargrave Road in 1938. For many years it was the home of Lakeland Laundry but the steady growth of Skipton Building Society saw them acquire the site. This 76 feet high block was put up in 1972 and has never been liked by Skiptonians. Indeed, they have royal backing for their views as Prince Charles, on a visit to Skipton, praised its architecture and character but famously took the Society to task for its concrete monolith. The then secretary of the society, H Taylforth, responding to criticisms of its height at the planning stage, commented: "It is unlikely that a modern office block in this particular position would spoil the visual amenity of the town." He then made the claim that it would not be seen from the High Street or Otley Street but there would be a "fleeting glimpse" from Court Lane. The building, however, dominates the townscape viewed from outside.

An interesting postscript from 1987 shows that local planners appear not to have forgiven Skipton Building Society and turned down an application for an illuminated sign on the front of the High Street branch. That led to what the council described as a "stroppy" letter from SBS and a decision to send an equally stroppy response. The society said that the same sign had been perfectly acceptable in historic Edinburgh; the council retorted that what was good enough for Edinburgh was not necessarily good enough for Skipton!

The society's headquarters moved to the Bailey in 1990, although this building is still used by parts of the society's empire, notably Home Loan Management. The building society continues to be a great success story in the financial world and the Bailey site at the time of writing was in the process of further building, an extension which would almost double the size of site and accommodate 1,400 employees.

Tucked away off Otley Street was the old British School opened in 1845 as a Congregational School. So-called British schools had opted out of the Church of England aligned National School system and were generally for Nonconformists. John Dewhurst dug deep into his pockets to provide much of the finance. Extended in 1856, one of its headmasters was Samuel Farey, of the mill owning family and it regularly received favourable reports from inspectors. It flourished until 1909 when the pupils were moved to Brougham Street.

The building then served for more than half a century as Thorneycroft's cabinet works but then it then fell vacant and the owners sought to demolish it for car parking. The council refused because of its historical and architectural value and the refusal was upheld on appeal to the Department of the Environment. The Civic Society had hopes of buying it at auction through public donations and using it for meetings, lectures and even small arts productions but its now occupied by printers Ellesmere Press.

Number 24 Otley Street was the home of the Kipling family after 1863. The Rev Joseph Kipling, grandfather of Rudyard Kipling, poet and author of the Jungle Book, was a Wesleyan Minister on the Skipton Circuit between 1860 and his death in 1862, living just round the corner in Alma Terrace. After his death the family moved to number 24 where his daughters Ruth and Jane ran a small school for young ladies of the town and that school was still in existence in 1885. The following year Frances, widow of Joseph, died and was buried alongside her husband in the cemetery on Raikes Road. Ruth Kipling then married George Dryden, clerk at Skipton Castle. As for the famous Rudyard, he is known to have spent several visits as a child to his aunts on Otley Street. Further down Otley Street lies the entrance to Craven Court.

If undertaken during the day, enter Craven Court via the ornate circular stairs. If locked, proceed along Otley Street to its junction with the High Street and turn left.

The fine award winning Craven Court complex was opened by television personality Michael Parkinson 1988, just a few weeks after a visit by Prince Charles to the nearly-completed building. In his book "A Vision of Britain" Prince Charles spoke highly of the development: "Craven Court is a new shopping centre. I rather like the way the developers have roofed over an old street and made it resemble an arcade. It's a bit like a covered market, which is very much a Yorkshire tradition".

In the past, however, Craven Court was simply a back street, off High Street. In 1930 Ledgard and Wynn moved into premises dealing with high class china and glass, furniture and carpets. Craven Court, originally Smith's Yard, was built by Mr Ralph Wynn in 1957 using doors and frames from old property in Skipton. He wanted it to resemble the Shambles in York. In 1986 Ledgard and Wynn moved to a new site on Chapel Hill and the property was bought by Estates and General Securities Ltd, who developed the area as a covered shopping centre and incorporated the old Hole in the Wall Inn, which had closed in 1986

Skipton 2000

A plaque announces the site of Skipton's first theatre, where once Edmund Keane trod the boards. In fact this theatre was in a yard off High Street behind the long-gone Hole in the Wall pub. The playhouse was nothing grand, being housed in a carpenter's workshop, and the leading promoter and actor was one Tom Airey, of Grassington, who had the monopoly of carrying mail between Upper Wharfedale and Skipton. Dawson recounts him leaving Skipton early in the morning in a lumbering stage coach drawn by two, (or in emergencies three) horses with a shrill blast on a long trumpet and resounding cracks of the whip, returning late in the evening. The stage was rudimentary and Dawson again tells a story of Airey's son holding a candle at arm's length behind a sheet of paper to depict a moon, only to set fire to the paper on one occasion, doubtless to the mirth of the audience.

"Airey's capacity as an actor was far from equal to his ambition," wrote Dawson, "yet he had a genuine passion for the footlights and left no possible expedient unregarded in his efforts to vie with large town theatres with unrestricted resources at their command." So he persuaded leading actors to head to Skipton, including Keane, though quite what they thought of playing a rudimentary theatre in a carpenter's shed behind a pub is anyone's guess.

Continue through Craven Court and back on to the High Street

Exiting Craven Court on to High Street, to the left is situated the Skipton branch of the Skipton Building Society, now a major financial institution which probably has supplied the mortgage for a majority of local homes. The Society was founded in 1853 at a meeting in the old Town Hall under the chairmanship of George Kendall. The report in the Craven Herald noted: "The benefits of building societies conducted on similar principles have, during the last few years been so fairly tested and so incontestably manifested that it is scarcely necessary for us to make any remarks on the subject; but satisfied as we are that the society (if properly managed) is calculated to confer lasting benefits on the town and neighbourhood, we cannot refrain not merely from bringing the matter before our readers but also of giving to its support that influence which the widely extending issues of the Herald allows us to impart." It described the building society's practice thus: "This society differs from the Old Building Societies in this, that it is not established for the express purpose of building a certain street, or row of houses, but what is much superior, it enables a man to build what he likes, where he likes and as he likes; or, if a member prefers to buy a building, he can do so and the society, if they think the purchase a good one, will advance the money; and if he wishes to neither build nor buy he will receive $4^{1}/_{2}$ per cent compound interest, calculated monthly and can withdraw at any time on giving a month's notice."

With this blessing the building society thrived. From its first office at Ship Corner it soon moved to 11 Newmarket Street in 1893, purchased at a cost of £300. In 1921 the company purchased 7 Newmarket Street but after only seven years this also was too small and the company moved to High Street. A year later its assets topped the £1 million mark. At first it operated from agency offices including church halls and village schools, open only on specified dates of the month. The first fully staffed full time branch was opened in Harrogate in 1947 and in 1962 its first outlet in the south, in Guildford was opened. It has swallowed up various other building societies, such as the Barnoldswick (in 1942), the Ribblesdale (1966), Bury (1974) and Otley (1982).

In 1928 the Building Society moved into the High Street in Skipton and as it expanded rapidly a new multi-storey office was built at the rear, between High Street and Court Lane. It still houses part of the Skipton Building Society business but in 1991 newer offices were built, this time just up the Bailey on the road to Harrogate. The society continued to succeed and in 1999 a further extension was under construction, due for completion in April 2000 as the Skipton-based workforce grew to more than 1,000. The Skipton remains fiercely determined to retain its mutual status in an age when many of its contemporaries have been swallowed up by, or converted into, companies owned by shareholders rather than members.

Next to Skipton Building Society is the Midland Bank, whose fine building was put up in 1888 and, to the right, Barclays Bank, built in 1849 and originally the Craven Bank. Formed in 1791, it is hard for us today to envisage a time when a local bank produced its own notes which, by all accounts were far more trusted in these parts than the Bank of England's! The founders of the Craven Bank were William and John Birkbeck, William Alcock, John Peart, Joseph Smith and William Lawson. The names are familiar to local historians as merchants, solicitors and manufacturers from the area who played a major role in the development of the commercial and indeed social aspects of the community. Back then bank notes were usually illustrated not with the sovereign's head but an emblem or picture of the town where it was based and so the Craven Bank adopted the famous Craven heifer on its currency and became known as

Skipton 2000

the notes "wi' t'cow on".

By 1880 the bank had seven branches and ten sub branches when it was decided that it should be incorporated as the Craven Bank Limited with an authorised capital of £1,200,000 divided into 40,000 shares of £30 each. Its head office moved from Settle to Skipton. The next few years were a period of branch expansion and increased profits but by the turn of the century the Craven Bank was struggling in a world of increasingly large and competitive banks so that in 1906 it amalgamated with the Bank of Liverpool. In deference to its traditions it was decided that its branches should continue to operate as an independent district within the Bank of Liverpool with Skipton as the district head office.

In 1918 there was another merger, this time the Bank of Liverpool joining with Martins Bank and in 1969 they amalgamated with Barclays. A history of Martins Bank, entitled Four Centuries of Banking, was written by a George Chandler and includes the memories of WB Carson who entered the Craven Bank head office in Skipton in 1898: "the strong room was lit by a gas jet and I remember on one occasion forgetting to turn off the gas before locking up. The room was very nearly airtight and on opening up the following day I found it full of gas and a long blue flame where the usual gas flame should have been. Expecting an immediate explosion, I and a fellow clerk bolted to the far end of the office and waited for it but nothing happened for a minute or two. I mustered up courage to run in and turn the gas off. Naturally, it was some time before the bank was clear of the smell of gas and I was told that it even reached the street. At that time gold was used by the Craven farmers to a great extent for the buying and selling of cattle and sheep and on a fair Monday there was quite a big turnover in it. The cattle market in Skipton was then held in the High Street and I remember on one or two occasions a cow managed to elude its owner or driver and get through the door into the customers' side of the bank counter. The half yearly balance used to be a pretty hectic affair in those days as a great deal of the work was left until the last day of the half year and the work often went on until about two o'clock in the morning. It was the custom then to stop work and the staff except the juniors used to partake of the directors' beer or whisky."

This was not the only bank based in Skipton. The Skipton Savings Bank was established in 1818 with the Duke of Devonshire and castle owner the earl of Thanet as patrons. It was attached to the post office and knew only one manager, Stephen Bailey Hall, who was something of a local poet. Hall was just 24 when he became manager at its inception and he was to remain in post until his death in 1866 when the bank perished with him

Just a little to the left, facing the High Street as one emerges from Craven Court, is the site of the Skipton's Market Cross where the opening of trading on market day was signalled by ringing the bell at the top of the structure. Geoffrey Rowley suggests that there may have been two market crosses, one indisputably outside the current Barclay's Bank, the other at the top end of the town to signify the corn market.

The market cross which is clearly recorded consisted, until it was taken down in 1840, of an awning under which farmers and others sold produce. It was built against a central pillar of stone surrounded by a tier of steps. All butter brought into town was weighed here and if any was found to be light weight it was given to the poor, who mustered in large numbers in eager anticipation.

Alongside stood the pillory, used for whipping miscreants for crimes such as robbery and sheep stealing. Sometimes the victim was tied to a cart and whipped down the High Street but a stationary punishment at the pillory was more common. In 1770 the pillory was removed but the stocks, outside Barclay's Bank, continued to be in use for another half century.

While on the topic of punishment, it is worth recounting a Skipton practice which may amuse modern readers. A beadle had been appointed by the Skipton magistrates in the early years of the 17th century because Skipton was "grievously pestered with rogues and vagabond persons that swarm in those parts more than in former times". The beadle's job was to round up the "foreign" beggars as the parish had quite enough poor of its own to look after and these interlopers were whipped and punished. A yearly sum of 26 shillings and eight pence had to be found to pay for the beadle's salary and anyone who refused to pay their contribution was to "taken bound to answeare his contempt in the p'misses at the next sessions". The image of a beadle conjures up to a modern audience the image of cinema versions of Dickens' Oliver Twist. Skipton's beadle seems to fit this image as he wore a cocked hat trimmed in gold and a matching coat and he carried with him a trident headed staff. By around 1800 he had another duty which reinforces the Dickens' image of an officious figure. At a certain stage during the Sunday church service the churchwardens and beadle withdrew and headed through the streets of the town. Should a person be found drunk in the streets or even drinking in one of the inns he was promptly escorted to the stocks and there impounded for the rest of the morning.

It is necessary to cross High Street again at the pedestrian crossing for the final section of the walk. This time turn left at the top of Middle Row, into Sheep Street, to conclude the walk at the Old Town Hall.

A row of shops at the south and west side of the High Street divides the main thoroughfare from Sheep Street. It is known as Middle Row but few would today agree with Dawson's comment of 1882 that "many wish that it [Skipton enterprise] may some day bring about the removal of the one defect of the magnificent market street, the block of buildings known as Middle Row. Perhaps the wish is a vain one."

The houses on Albert Street, a throughfare off to the right from Sheep Street as one heads towards the old town hall, were demolished in 1955 but these were not slums, instead they were beautifully restored and a sit-in protest made the national headlines. Also destroyed was the last detached Georgian House in Skipton. An appeal in court against its demolition was refused and Harry Myers, the owner, refused to demolish the property. The council broke in and sold off the dressed stone in an act of official vandalism which still rankled many years later. Sir John Betjeman came to photograph the house in 1956 in his national survey of buildings and was horrified to find it had been flattened. Incredibly the area was not developed until 30 years later. The site of Devonshire House was replaced by a barn like structure used by a printing firm, then became Hillard's, Skipton's first supermarket before more modern buildings were finally put up in the 1980s.

A feature of the inside of WH Smith's shop is the Minstrel's Gallery which goes unnoticed by many customers. A glance upwards inside the shop entrance will show the feature, whose origin is unknown. Dr Rowley wrote: What the source of the minstrel's gallery legend is I do not know but I find it odd that neither Whitaker or Dawson mention it since most of Sheep Street dates from 1790 or so. I think it is unlikely that the building is old enough to have a minstrel's gallery or that any family in Skipton was important enough to boast such an extravagance except occupants of the castle." Yet a similar gallery exists in the building now occupied by Clinton's Cards but, alas, has been hidden from view

The old town hall was the site of the court leet which enforced public order in the town. It was here that smallholders who allowed their animals to stray, traders who, in the modern parlance "ripped off" the public and nuisances who disturbed the peace were dealt with. The court leet also saw that roads were kept in good repair and market customs were upheld. Woe betide the person caught giving light weight in selling food stuffs. Fines went straight into the coffers of the lord of the manor. Some examples of the decisions passed down include:

"We the jurymen, do amerce (fine) the several persons who ought to repair the highway leading from Skipton within this manor to Drafton, to witt, from a place called Skipton Schooll Bridge to a place within this manner called Witchhole the sum of thirteen shillings and four pence.

"We the jurymen do amerce each p'son who shall hereafter suffer their hogs or swine to go at large within the jurisdiction of this court the sum of 3s 4d for each hog or swine."

These examples date from the 18th century and there are others: fines for allowing horses to remain in the street on market days, keeping mastiff dogs at large and unmuzzled in the town, not cutting grass, selling a bull without it being baited.

These early courts were concerned mainly with regulating markets and trading in the town but they became increasingly involved in cases public nuisance. Court records of April 3 1743 refer to an Abraham Dixon, who owned land alongside Waller Beck off Newmarket Street, as washing wool and disposing of animal remains in the stream. There are numerous instances of householders being brought before the court for keeping dunghills and rubbish tips outside their homes. For example, on April 25 1804 "Jane Cork, of Skipton, widow, has occasioned a nuisance at sundry times by emptying the contents of chamber pots and throwing dish washings etc into the streets of Skipton". On October 18 1748 the court heard that the landlord of the George Inn, one William Howson, "and the occupier of his slaughter house do permit blood and other offals and unwholesome garbage to run and be taken into the streets". The court could impose fines and there seems an air of frustration about it in October 1741 when it ordered a fine of 6s 8d for every inhabitant if they did not "from time to time clean their fronts of dirt".

Until 1856 there was a lock up cell underneath the Town Hall. Dawson described it as "very dark, damp and badly ventilated. It was a vile place in which to confine any human being whatever his offence." Conditions for women prisoners were much better, the cell being approached from High Street rather than being subterranean. When a police station was built in Middletown there was no longer a need for the lock-ups.

The walk has ended, outside the old Skipton Town Hall.

Appendix 1: The Guy Fawkes Riot

November 5 1874 saw scenes in Skipton which seem amazing to the modern inhabitants of this small, conservative, market town in the Yorkshire Dales. Police attacks with drawn truncheons on stone throwing rioters in the streets suggests an inner city riot of the modern era rather than our Victorian forebears. The following account is based upon the report in the Craven Pioneer which described the event as "notable in the annals of Skipton for there has been disgrace thrown upon the town which cannot be removed by mere words". Far from upholding the forces of law and order, it was heavily critical of the superintendent of police, Thomas Grisdale: "Almost universal indignation has been uttered against the action of the police and more especially towards the superintendent, Mr Grisdale....Guy Fawkes day has always been commemorated in Skipton with a large expenditure of gunpowder but there never was an instance to equal the riotous conduct on Tuesday and it is an undoubted fact that the inhabitants of the town attribute the disturbance entirely to the police."

The trouble started when Supt Grisdale posted notices around the town warning against the setting off of fireworks in public places, especially the High Street, and his intention to ensure such scenes did not occur. On November 5 the inhabitants noticed a large number of policemen patrolling the streets as reinforcements had been brought in from villages all around, swelling the normal ranks of five constables in the town to 25. Word got round that something was to happen at by 7.30 there were large crowds on the High Street. At intervals, squibs and crackers were set off by mischievous youths, to cheers from bystanders and the frustration of the police who appeared powerless to stop the scenes.

"As the night wore on, the crowds of spectators still increased and the police became more obtrusive, evidently incensed by the failure of their endeavours. instead of contenting themselves with ascertaining the names of such of the culprits as they could secure, they commenced an insane attempt to clear the streets," wrote the Pioneer. "Persons quietly walking on the causeways were interrupted, shouldered and ordered to go back and this course of conduct, very exasperating and injudicious, and perhaps as illegal, led on to the more serious fracas."

The trouble escalated when the policemen drew their truncheons and attacked the crowd. Respectable traders were knocked to the floor, women were shaken and others struck.

"What led the police to do this we cannot tell," said the Pioneer. "It has been stated that stones were thrown at them, but this statement is generally denied; neither did our reporter see any and, even if there were, it could not justify the police in reckless attacks upon the people."

The attacks led to groans, hisses and abuse poured upon Supt Grisdale and more charges into the crowd, which showed itself to be most reluctant to disperse.

Around 10 o'clock a drum and fife band appeared and made its way to Sheep Street where it played God Save the Queen and Auld Lang Syne. This seemed to quieten matters and about an hour later, it all seemed to be over. It wasn't. For some reason the violence flared up again, perhaps because people who had not turned out earlier were coming into town to search for their loved ones and were swelling the crowd. Stones began to be thrown in large numbers at the unfortunate policemen, who were forced to seek refuge. They regrouped and then charged with "terrible vigour", dealing out their blows "without discrimination of age or sex". Windows were broken and many of the policemen were injured by stones.

"Although we have been unable to obtain many names of persons injured, doubtless there are many who will long remember the hurts they received," commented the Pioneer. Those who were hurt included an 82-year-old John Tomlinson, thrown to the ground and Marshall Banks, cut on the head by a truncheon who had his hands in his pockets watching the riot unfold.

Several respectable inhabitants were named as falling foul of the police violence.

Not that the police were unscathed and Supt Grisdale himself was cut on the thigh, legs and back. He had been hit on the head with a stone and his hat shattered. Among the injured policemen was PC Limb, carried into the Hole in the Wall pub with a severe cut on the head and in a fainting condition.

The following day the scenes of the riot were plain for all to see on the streets and a further 80 police reinforcements were drafted in from all over the West Riding under the command of the chief constable. That night a "number of roughs" gathered at Manby's Corner and set off a few fireworks but JB Dewhurst "kindly advised them to go home and not be the means of causing any offence". Supt Grisdale, whenever he was spotted, was "received with such marks of disapprobation as to show plainly that his presence was disadvantageous to order and peace". There then appears to have been a sort of negotiation on the street in which Mr Dewhurst and the chief constable heard the grievances of the townsfolk. It looked ominous for the beleaguered superintendent when he was sent home. The heavy police presence and the disappearance of Supt Grisdale calmed things down and there was no trouble.

That week's Pioneer carried a stinging letter from a clearly well-educated and prominent person who hid behind the identity of "Sub Lege Libertas". It raged: "All who witnessed the outrageous and imperious manner in which he sought not to prevent or detect parties letting off fireworks etc but to over-ride and trample upon the liberties of the people could not but conclude that if any person was responsible for the breach of the peace, that person was the superintendent....Some of the most inoffensive inhabitants of the town were subjected to very rough and insolent usage by the police who charged indiscriminately with drawn truncheons and not infrequently both women and children were roughly handled and struck at by these guardians (!) of the peace."

The letter continued: "Our superintendent seems to have thought himself strong enough to stamp out a custom that has existed for over two and a half centuries. Poor man!". It called for his instant removal from the post. A week later, that call was to be granted.

A few days later the reckoning came in court when Skipton men apprehended were drawn before the bench. When Supt Grisdale made his entrance into the court room he was greeted with obvious signs of displeasure from a packed courthouse. Whistles and hisses rang out from the public benches.

Mr Ferns, prosecuting, told the bench how the superintendent had arranged for bills to be printed and posted on the streets of Skipton warning against discharging fireworks on the street. Defending was a Mr Turner, who said, to applause, that he was sad to state that had it not been for the conduct of Supt Grisdale then no disturbance would have taken place.

First up was a Joseph Barker, a quarryman who was fined 20 shillings for throwing a stone, despite his protestations of innocence. The decision was greeted with boos and hisses from the public. He was followed by William Baldwin, who was fined the same amount upon the same charge. This time the chairman of the bench, our old friend Mathew Wilson, commented that "any person who was there was liable just as much as the defendant and referred to it being almost impossible for any policeman to distinguish in such a crowd very many of those who threw stones" – a curious legal argument and one which drew hisses from the court.

Ovington Butler was the next charged and among the witnesses was Supt Grisdale, who was hissed as he got to his feet. He said that he had come into Caroline Square when he was struck by a firework thrown from a house. Policemen were complaining that stones were being thrown at them and he therefore went in front of the crowd and told them not to be so cowardly. Cross-examined, the superintendent denied that he had struck anyone and denied that a policeman had thrown the first stone. Butler was fined 20 shillings, as was the next defendant, Abraham Varley.

The next accused was a John Thomas Parkinson on a different charge, that of assaulting a policeman. Despite the denials, the routine was by now clearly set – fined 20 shillings.

Next up was Thomas Phillips, a draper, charged with setting off a firework but he did not appear in the court, sending a message that it was a busy day for him and could he be dealt with in his absence. The prosecutor, Mr Ferns, asked for a warrant to be issued immediately and for Phillips to be brought in front of the magistrates. Perhaps sensing the ugly mood of the public, or perhaps with a little common sense dawning, Supt Grisdale defused the situation by offering to withdraw the charge upon the payment of costs, a compromise which the bench accepted with alacrity.

The next case was unusual, in that John Staveley brought a summons against PC Metcalfe of assault. The ordinary townsman claimed that he was caught up in the disturbance after returning from the railway station. He was making his way to his home in Chancery Lane (now Court Lane) when he arrived in Caroline Square. He had seen no disturbance and saw no reason why he should turn back when all he wanted to do was go home. This refusal to turn round, he alleged, led PC Metcalfe to assault him. Mr Ferns told the court that the policeman had no case to answer. He had been directed to clear the streets in order to observe the peace and in doing so the complainant had refused to give way and been knocked to the ground. The magistrates had to decide if more force had been used than was necessary. It will come as little surprise that the magistrates dismissed the case.

This again enraged the general public watching affairs and hisses and boos broke out. Suddenly Grisdale, who according to the report had said nothing at previous disturbances, jumped to his feet, stood on the bench and shouted out: "Constables, the first man who creates a noise or disturbance you must take into custody. This court must not be kept in a continual disturbance". The report was followed by "uproar and more hisses" but the report does not state that anyone was apprehended. Indeed the proceedings were more or less over. Mathew Wilson made the comment that fireworks were dangerous and improper in the streets; "the town had become too great and too important to admit of such childish practices" and he called for arrangements for fireworks to be let off elsewhere so there might not be such danger of setting fire to buildings or injuring persons.

And that was the end of the affair. Supt Grisdale was on his way virtually as soon as the court proceedings were over and the town returned quickly to normality. It seems as though the incident did ensure the end of bonfires and fireworks in the High Street for no further mention is made of the practice and old Skiptonians have no recollection of any celebration of Guy Fawkes Day in the streets.

Appendix 2: School life in Skipton

SCHOOL days of yore are often viewed as the good old days, when reading, writing and arithmetic ruled and dedicated staff taught eager pupils. But was this the real story? A fascinating account of school life at the turn of the century is detailed in the minute book kept by two head teachers at Water Street school. Its pages unveil a story of sickness epidemics, poor working conditions, absenteeism among staff and a head teacher struggling to cope with the system.

The story is taken up first by the headmaster, Mr WH Walker, who records important items such as a school inspection, unusual levels of absenteeism, new teachers etc. The first entry, dated July 24 1902, details that attendance of the 706 pupils is down due to sickness. This is to be recurring theme as we reproduce extracts from the fascinating working life of this school:

1902

September 8: Mr Walker notes that 38 children are absent on the first day back at school after the holidays. The following day he has an explanation: 20 have gone on to work without him being informed and several have left the town!

September 18: An insight into working hours as the minute book notes sternly: "Miss Irving is frequently very late when she should sit with the pupil teachers during their instruction. This morning she came in at 8.10 instead of 7.45."

December 16: "I have found it necessary to punish several boys severely for smoking cigarettes and have decided to dismiss T Brade."

1903

February 27 1903: A "terrible gale" hits Skipton. As a result 116 children are absent. Later, on March 20, it so wet that over 100 children fail to turn up for school in the afternoon. The rest are sent home.

May 12: It's not just the children who fail to turn up. The book notes that for the first time since the school reopened after Easter on April 20 all 11 teachers have reported for work!

July 27: A measles epidemic strikes and more than 100 children are absent. "The work in such conditions is exceedingly depressing" notes the headmaster.

September 21: Attendance at Water Street is much improved but the epidemic appears to have taken a firm grip in the town as Mr Walker notes that several other schools have been forced to close.

November 13: Mr Walker announces that "due to the state of my health" he is to instruct his junior teachers at his (unspecified) home address at the usual time of 7.45am! The health of Mr Walker is to feature later in the log book.

1904

February 23: Attendance among teachers is so bad that an exasperated Mr Walker notes that he is finding it extremely difficult to work the school. The measles epidemic rages on and the local medical officer orders the closure of the infants school.

February 29: "I feel rather discouraged with the attendance. It is certainly a very cold morning but there is little snow. Yet we have 86 children absent. Of these 18 have been kept at home through measles and one through fever. "

March 18: A hint of class sizes. Mr Walker notes that in the first class 34 children are present and 26 absent. He comments: "There is much indifference among parents as to the education of their children".

April 1: The new Education Act of 1902 came into force. The book states that this meant that from now on the school came under the control of the new authority – West Riding County Council based at Wakefield.

May 11: Mr Walker announces his return to school after four weeks off due to "severe haemorrhage from the lungs". Deputy head Mr Burniston has taken charge.

May 17: Three children are discovered to have ringworm, three fever and one diphtheria.

June 14: Mr Walker again laments the poor attendance, noting that on average 50 children are absent every time the school is open.

June 30: Things are not going well with the new education authority. Teacher Miss Ellen Holmes has left but no steps have been taken to replace her. Mr Walker is forced to take over her duties.

July 7: "The attendance officer called this morning. The strain is almost intolerable" is the entry in the log book.

July 14: Still no replacement for Miss Holmes.

July 19: 65 children are noted absent. Again Mr Walker berates parents: "This is very bad. People are very indifferent and careless re the attendance of their children at school".

July 25: Mr Walker again notes that no-one has been taken on to replace Miss Holmes, adding that she handed in her notice in mid-May. His problems are about to get worse. On July 28 another teacher, Miss Edmondson, leaves.

August 29: School reopened after the summer holidays - but without a replacement for the two teachers who have left. According to the board of education's minimum scale, the school has staff for 410 pupils. Attendance was given right at the start of the log book as 706.

September 16: An inspector's report is written down, starting with the comment that there are still no replacement teachers. The report states: "The premises have been added to from time to time and are not very convenient and several of the classes are very large. It does not seem desirable that so many children should be be taught in these premises and, owing to the size of the classes, more certificated teachers should be employed. Nothing but the good discipline and able organisation of the school could render possible the level of attainments reached. As the boys in two of the classrooms have to pass through the girls' cloakroom to reach the playground, they should be dismissed before or after the girls. The playgrounds are small."

October 11: The school is closed owing to the visit in town of "Buffalo Bill".

October 14: The beleaguered head appears close to breaking point. He notes in the log book: "I really haven't the time to do the clerical work necessary and proper supervision of the school is out of the question. The teachers are working hard and doing their best to help me but the work is intolerable, or at least the conditions under which we work are intolerable".

October 24: Another teacher, Miss Greenwood, hands in her notice stating that her salary is unsatisfactory.

November 21: A red letter day. At long last a replacement teacher starts.

1905

February 9: A report on the school exams and the head admits his disappointment. "Throughout the school mental arithmetic seems weak and the girls are careless and indifferent". The blame is put on the shortage of staff and the high level of absenteeism among both pupils and teachers.

February 14: A boy, F Gallagher, is expelled from the school for "sheer impudence".

March 31: More dissatisfaction with the new education authority. The head is required to hang up a timetable in the school. He has rearranged classes but the day before the new school year (on April 1), his scheme of work has not arrived, nor has approval for his plans been received despite being posted to county hall seven weeks earlier.

April 3: The first day of a new school year and 10 teachers are in charge of 458 pupils. One of the teachers, a Mr Carruthers, has an unspecified illness and will be absent for many weeks.

September 4: The school reopens after the summer holidays with three new pupil teachers - Kate Lancaster, Agnes Lawrie and Robert Holmes - but there is a sting in the tail!

November 2: The student teachers inform Mr Walker that, having completed 100 days in the junior school, they must continue their training at the Skipton Girls' Endowed School. Mr Walker notes: "It is a strange thing that the headmaster should receive instruction through his pupil teachers. It seems as though he was no longer the head of his school."

November 3: A change to the administration of the school. It is no longer run from West Riding headquarters in Wakefield but passed to the hands of local managers on the Skipton Education Sub-Committee.

1906

January 8: Despite the change in organisation, the pupil teachers remain at the Girls' School. They are not due to return until 1907.

January 12: The log book starkly notes that the headmaster has tendered his resignation. It will take effect on March 31. All subsequent entries are in the hand of the deputy, Mr Asa Burniston. At first one assumes that the pressure of staff shortages has driven Mr Walker to despair.

March 31: The last day of the school year, and the last day at school of Mr Walker. No comment other than that he finished his duties, is made in the log book. It is the last day of another teacher, Miss Ramsden and Mr Burniston states: "As far as I know, no-one is coming to take the place of either".

April 2: The new school year starts with 458 children on the register and eight teachers. A Mr George Langley is announced as the new head, but it is unlikely that he will take up his duties for some time.

May 7: George Langley arrives as headmaster. Among his first entries is to note that he will also spend some time at Carleton while a new headmaster is appointed there.

November 8: More light is shed on what appeared to be the sudden departure of Mr Walker. Mr Langley notes that the school is closed for the afternoon "to allow teachers and scholars to attend the funeral of the late Mr WH Walker, late headmaster of this school". Recalling Mr Walker's two absences due to severe haemorrhaging from the lungs, perhaps his resignation was due less to the pressure than his ill health.

November 8: On the same day as Mr Walker's funeral, Mr Langley records that he has been selected to tour America as part of the "Mosely Commission" for six weeks, leaving the following day.

November 12: Broughton Road School is closed due to diphtheria for a week and teacher Miss Gertrude Smith is temporarily transferred to Water Street.

1907

January 7: Mr Langley returns from his visit to the United States.

January 25: Mr Langley institutes a new system under which each class has to recite quotations on one special day each week. The head notes that the school is very cold, with some classrooms being as low as 47 degrees.

February 28: A school report. General attainments are creditable but the inspector strikes a sour note: "Whispering in Standard VI should be discouraged and the children in Standard I are inclined to jump up in their eagerness to answer".

March: Throughout the month there is a problem of absenteeism with regular entries for staff being away. One, Miss Kellett, has been absent from October and will only return in April, her illness unspecified.

April 19: Miss Ada Blanche Young is appointed school monitor on a salary of £7 per year.

1908

April 16: The school closes for two weeks due to an outbreak of measles.

When it reopens, 115 of the 365 pupils are off sick. A visit by the medical officer takes place on May 6 and he closes the school down. It does not reopen until June 15.

September 23: A new outbreak, this time of scarlet fever.

October 2: "A copy of the regulations on corporal punishment was received this morning and was read out to the whole staff with a request that they should be strictly adhered to. The following certificated assistants of over three years experience were delegated the power to inflict corporal punishment to boys for grave offences. Miss Thornton, Miss Ramsden, Mr Burniston, Mr Hill. In no case was power delegated for the corporal punishment of girls and I expressly forbade such punishment".

October 5: Teacher Mr Boyes is absent from school. "No reason has been given although he was seen in Skipton today".

1909

March 5: A visit from the medical officer owing to an outbreak of scarlet fever. He recommends careful watching for discharge from nose or ears from returned patients.

March 12: Two girls are excluded from school because they have ringworm.

April 23: A school report is favourable in tone. It notes that a school library has been formed and is well supplied. Excursions have been noted for nature study and more are encouraged.

November 23: "Mr Thornton brought word that owing to the necessity of lessening the number of classes in the main room, Miss Binns would be required to resign on December 1".

1910

March 18: The deputy head, Mr Burniston, leaves to take over as headmaster at Rainhall Road school in Barnoldswick.

July 20: In line with inspectors' recommendations, excursions are held to Bolton Abbey and Barden Towers.

September 27: On instructions from West Riding, lessons are given on temperance.

October 25: Despite cold weather, swimming competitions are held at Moorview open air baths. It is reported that 12 children qualified for a certificate, 12 could swim a length on the breast and three on the back - a small number given the size of the school.

1911

February 13: The school reopens after Christmas and is immediately closed for five weeks by the medical officer as there is an outbreak of scarlet fever. it reopened with an attendance of 258, with Mr Langley personally inspecting the arms of each child for signs of 'peeling'. There are no suspicious cases.

October 3: A doctor visits the school to examine a child who has had two fits in school. The child is subsequently excluded owing to him being subject to epileptic fits.

1912

February 5: Severe weather and the school suffers from inadequate heating. The gases are burnt during the day as an absolute necessity. Temperature in the main room at 9am is just 44 degrees.

March 19: Mr Langley records his absence from school due to the illness of his wife.

March 26: A stoic report from the headmaster: "I have been away from school since the 19th owing to the illness and death of my wife (March 20)".

September 9: Following on from the problems with the school heating, a new boiler has been installed and four new radiators put into the main room and two into each classroom over the summer break.

1913

July 11: Brougham Street school closes due to an outbreak of mumps. It spreads through the town and Water Street school follows on July 16.

July 24: An inspector's report states: "The distinguishing feature of this school is the provision that is made for the education of the older scholars by means of an advanced class. The headmaster secures the co-operation of the parents who undertake, as a rule, that the children shall remain at school either the whole or a definite part of the course instead of leaving when entitled to do so by age. Private study is encouraged and the desire to become a member of the advanced class proves a healthy stimulus and the fact that it fulfils a definite need and is appreciated is attested by the fact that a number of children attend it from a considerable distance." The report said that the premises need to be cleaned and decorated throughout, with lighter colours recommended. The inspector also notes what appears to be an example of pre-First World War graffiti: "At 9am on Monday morning the walls were covered with writing and drawings of a highly objectionable character which were evidently quite freshly done. No blame of course can possibly attach to the head teacher".

1914

January: The year opens with yet another enforced closure, this time due to measles. It reopens in February.

April 23: The funeral takes place of the headmistress of the school's infant department. No explanation is given.

May 4: Following a visit from a Mr Raeburn and Miss Gill, 80 children had dental operations.

December 14: The first one of very few references to the First World War. The war office has taken over some of the schools in Skipton and it is noted that the Water Street premises will be used by two schools, Water Street pupils taking over from 8.30am to 12.30pm, the National School (Parish Church) from 1pm to 5pm.

1915

January 29: Normality is resumed and the National School moves back to its normal premises.

August 27: A teacher, Miss Thornton, is away from school after she receives news that her brother has died of wounds in Flanders.

November 17: Mr Langley is absent as he is Draughton, Bolton Abbey, Arncliffe, Halton Gill and Penyghent for a recruiting drive "under Lord Derby's scheme".

November 29: Teacher Mr Hill enlists in the army under Lord Derby's scheme.

1916

May 3: Special lessons were given to mark the tercentenary of William Shakespeare.

May 24: The afternoon was devoted to the celebration of Empire Day. A special address on our duties to the Empire was given and patriotic songs, recitations and quotations were given by the children.

November 28: The school boiler bursts and school is closed for two weeks.

1917

May 24: Entries in the log book become increasingly infrequent. Empire Day is celebrated again, this time the teachers gave talks on "our duties to the Empire, especially under present circumstances. Stress was laid on rationing". However references to the war are virtually non-existent, even though many, if not virtually all, the pupils must have suffered the loss of a family relative.

June 13: Mr Langley attends the funeral of Mr Fred Metcalfe, "an old schol-

ar of Carleton who died of wounds".
1918
January 29: Frequent absences from school by the headmaster Mr Langley are finally explained. He suffered from sciatica.

June 3: An outbreak of measles closes the school.

July 3: A teacher, Alfred Pawson, collapses while instructing the boys on swimming lessons with Mr Langley. He is sent home in a cab. He returns later, only to leave the school on September 6.

November 1: An influenza outburst closes the school. It is due to reopen on November 11 – Armistice Day. However the school remains closed until January 6 due to the influenza outbreak which is to claim the lives of many people in the wake of the First World War.
1919
June 19: The school is closed to honour the return of the commander of the 1/6 West Riding Regiment.

July 11: The school does not open until 1pm due to the arrival in Skipton of "Wombell's Menagerie" – as mentioned in Caroline Square, chapter 11. Meanwhile Mr Langley's illness continues, reporting himself absent on no less than five occasions between October 3 and December 18.
1920
January 21: The headmaster is absent for 14 days during the month with illness.

May 3: The first inspector's report since the outbreak of war notes that book keeping and shorthand have been included on the curriculum but the latter should be discontinued as it is unsuitable to the children's requirements. Easy exercises in arithmetic were reported as not being well done.

November 8: "Owing to children attending some of the mills not being able to reach school by 1.15 it has been decided to return to the usual time of opening school, viz 1.30 in the afternoon".
1921
November 1: An inspector praises the school for its pleasing state of efficiency. Staff and headmaster work zealously and instruction is carried out on sensible and thorough lines. The children are interested and eager and arithmetic results are well above average
1922
September 29: The final entry in the log book. It states: "In accordance with

instructions from West Riding County Council, this school is reorganised as a junior school (infants, and standards I and II) from October 1 under the supervision of Miss Barber from the infants' department and my connection with the school ceases".

No indication or explanation of the reorganisation is made and what became of Mr Langley is unclear.

What is clear is that Water Street did continue, establishing itself as a strong, popular school within Skipton.

Appendix 3: Some notable Skiptonians

TIMOTHY CROWTHER

IN the mid 18th century Timothy Crowther was the parish clerk of the town but he was more famous around the county of Yorkshire for being an astrologer able to foretell events and a man able to cast out evil spirits and overturn charms. The expression "as cunning as Crowther" was well known in Skipton a century after his death, giving an indication of what the locals thought of him. Perhaps the incident of the church bells explains why he achieved such a reputation.

Crowther had, for some reason, become dissatisfied with the peal of bells at Holy Trinity and complained that they were cracked and not good enough for a town of Skipton's importance so he asked the churchwardens for a new set. The proposal was out of the question for the parsimonious wardens, particularly those who lived out of the town and would benefit less but Crowther modified his request, asking for permission to order a new set of clappers which was duly adhered to. So large were the clappers that he ordered that the first time they were used on the bells there could be no disputing the damage caused and the bells were clearly cracked. The changing was no longer optional but compulsory. The parish register of 1757 shows the bells being out of repair and in 1759 the township decided to purchase new ones, at the heavy cost of £293.

A measure of his reputation is given in John Wesley's Journal. In the entry dated July 24 1761 he recounts a visit to Bramley where a teenager called John Rushforth told him of a visit he had made to Mr Crowther of Skipton to clear up the mysterious disappearance of a man. Crowther had refused to speak to friends and neighbours, insisting that a boy of 12 or 13 should see him. Rushforth accordingly went to Skipton for a consultation and Crowther gave him a looking glass, asking what he saw in its reflection. The boy saw the missing man, drunk, in an alehouse near Bradford pulling out a guinea, watched by a big man and a small man. The missing neighbour was then ambushed, killed by these two and his body thrown into a coal pit. The boy then went on to relate how a party went to the spot seen in the boy's vision and indeed found the missing man, murdered.

Wesley is dismissive: "Is it improbable only or flatly impossible when all the circumstances are considered that this should be all pure fiction? They that can believe this may believe a man's getting in a bottle."

In 1771 the churchwardens attempted to get rid of Crowther on account of his drunken behaviour, an incident related fully in the chapter on Holy Trinity

Crowther left a handwritten book of his life, in particular his astrological charts and signs to look for in forecasting the weather and detailed accounts of how to exorcise evil spirits

WILLIAM HARBUTT DAWSON

BORN in Skipton in 1860, Dawson's legacy was to pass on to future generations the most scholarly history of the town, a book which remains the standard source today. His middle name comes from his maternal uncle, who invented plasticine, known originally as Harbutt's Plasticine.

His father, John, had founded a temperance newspaper, the Craven Pioneer (later to merge with the Craven Herald) and he started in the office after leaving Ermysted's. A scholarly man he trawled through documents in Skipton Castle and in the Petyt Library to publish his History of Skipton in 1882. His diaries relate how he did the research from 5am in the morning, then went to his desk at the Pioneer, before returning to his scholastic task until late into the night. Sixty years later he was to revise his work and sold the copyright to the Craven Herald. Alas, despite some plaintive letters to the Herald just after the Second World War, he was not to live to see his work completed. A letter from the Herald describes how paper rationing prevented its publication and it was not until 1972 that the second edition of his book was published by the Herald.

Dawson did not remain long in Skipton after his History was published. He moved to a newspaper in the West Country and soon after to Paris, working on a Berlin newspaper published in English! He became editor of this paper and studied at Berlin University, writing two further books - German Socialism and Ferdinand Lassalle and Bismarck and State Socialism.

Upon the death of his father he returned to Skipton to take over as editor of the Pioneer and was active in establishing the Cottage Hospital (Granville Street). His academic work continued and his writings on Social Reform led to a visit back to Germany on behalf of David Lloyd George to study social insurance. This was to lead to him becoming a secretary to Lloyd George and a close involvement with the 1910 National Insurance Act, which was the first provision for sickness and unemployment payment. He took early retirement to Beckenham, in Kent, later to Oxford, to write books and articles. Their titles include Problems of the Peace, Evolution of Modern Germany, The German Empire and Richard Cobden and Foreign Policy.

He was also greatly interested in the Civil War and wrote a book on General John Lambert, from Calton, entitled Cromwell's Understudy. Some Civil War relics he collected, such as a sword blade, a cannon ball and tinder box were left to the Craven Museum in his home town

CHRISTOPHER SIDGWICK

THE name of Sidgwick, and in particular Christopher Sidgwick, crops up throughout the Victorian history of the town. It was in 1785 that High Mill in Skipton Woods was opened in a partnership between a John Sidgwick, his brother in law Peter Garforth and John Blackburn. Sidgwick was already in business as a cotton spinner in Bingley and it seems that the Skipton business was run by his son, William, who was to marry Ann Benson. The couple built and lived in Stone Gappe at Lothersdale and after William's death, the widow lived at the gatehouse to Skipton Castle.

It is with their son, John Benson Sedgwick, that the family becomes of great interest because he had three sons, Benson, William and Christopher, and their governess at their Lothersdale home was none other than novelist Charlotte Bronte, from Haworth. Indeed, her book Jane Eyre drew upon her experiences in the household and the Gateshead Hall of the book is reckoned to be Stone Gappe and the character Mrs Read was taken to be Mrs Sidgwick. The book displeased the Sidgwick family and there appears to have been a frosty relationship. This is captured in a letter Charlotte wrote to Emily in 1839: "The children are constantly with me and more riotous, perverse, unmanageable cubs never grew." She referred to the mother: "I now begin to find that she does not intend to know me, that she cares nothing in the world about me, except to contrive how the greatest quantity of labour may be squeezed out of me". Charlotte Bronte was better disposed towards the master of the house: "Mr Sidgwick walked out with his children and I had orders to follow a little behind. As he strolled through the fields with his magnificent Newfoundland dog at his side, he looked very like what a frank, wealthy Conservative gentleman ought to be."

A relative, AC Benson, writing a biography of another Sidgwick relative who was to become Archbishop of Canterbury, Archbishop Edward White Benson, puts the family view: "Charlotte Bronte acted as governess to my cousins at Stone Gappe for a few months in 1839. Few traditions of her connection with the Sidgwicks survive. She was, according to her own account, very unkindly treated but it is clear that she had no gifts for the management of children and was also in a very morbid condition the whole of the time. My cousin, Benson Sidgwick, certainly on one occasion threw a Bible at Miss Bronte and all that another cousin can recollect of her is that if she was invited to walk to church with them, she thought she was being ordered about like a slave; if she was not invited, she imagined that she was cut off from the family circle. Both Mr and Mrs Sidgwick were extraordinarily benevolent people, much beloved, and would not willingly have given pain to anyone connected with them."

JB Sidgwick, and his brother Robert, built the Low Mill in Sackville Street in 1839 while his second son, William, became a clergyman and master at Ermysted's. It was the third son whose story now interests us. In 1833, at the age of 29, he gave up full time working in the family mill business and was instrumental in the building and endowment of the new Christ Church, the first in Craven to be built since the Reformation.

Shortly after Christ Church was completed, he turned his attention to education and built the single storey building on Water Street which served as a school for the children at the Sidgwick Mills. When the new Christ Church school was opened in 1844, the pupils transferred there. Sidgwick was to become, briefly, head of the new Parish Church School in Otley Street but left in a disagreement over whether its Sunday School scholars should attend service at Holy Trinity or his beloved Christ Church. Sidgwick next appears in 1858 when the Skipton

Local Board of Health was formed. This body was the precursor of the council, its duties to supervise sanitary conditions in the town. These duties were wide, including sanitation, drains, roads, water supply, gas supply, so that eventually it was to become, in effect, "the council" before the Local Government Act created Skipton Urban District Council in 1897. The Local Board was set up after an application and subsequent inquiry to the General Board of Health into the need for a Skipton Local Board.

There were 30 nominees for election to the first board, nine declined to serve and so an election was held for the nine places. The poll was topped by Henry Alcock with Robert Hodgson Sidgwick (Christopher's uncle) was runner-up. Also elected was John Bonny Dewhurst, Mark Scott of the brewery family and, last of the nine, Christopher Sidgwick. Alcock was the first chairman and when he stepped down, Christopher took over and was in the chair from 1862 to 1870. He was to die in 1877. In 1908 the Craven Herald marked the 50th anniversary of the Local Board and published a picture of each of the chairmen save Sidgwick, remarking that he "unfortunately had a rooted objection to facing the camera and there is no portrait of him extant".

Sidgwick's good works in the town dragged him into the affair of the statue of Sir Mathew Wilson, outlined in the first chapter of this book. When the Liberals started their campaign for the still living Sir Mathew to be honoured by a statue, the Craven Herald, indignantly put forward the claims of Christopher Sidgwick, who had been dead some 10 years. It became a bitterly political argument, with Sir Mathew winning due perhaps to the fact that Liberal supporters in Bradford were willing to dig into their pockets, while the more parsimonious Skiptonians were less enthusiastic about committing their funds to a statue.

SIR MATHEW WILSON

SIR Mathew's name has cropped up throughout the book. Skipton even put up a statue to him while he was still alive although it seems as though the bulk of the money came from his friends in Bradford.

Wilson was born in 1802 and died on January 18 1891 at his residence in Brighton from bronchitis. An obituary of the time states that the flag at the Bradford Liberal Club was lowered to half mast when the news came through and the statue in Skipton was draped in a wreath. He was a local man, born at

Eshton Hall, eldest son of Mathew and Margaret Wilson, who were cousins. It was a wealthy family and the young Mathew was sent to Harrow and from there went to Brasenose College, Oxford. He married in 1826, Sophia Louisa Emerson, and the couple had a child, Mathew Wharton Wilson, who was born the following year. Sophia was to die at Kildwick Hall in 1833.

In 1824, at the age of 22, he was made a magistrate, probably the youngest in the West Riding and at the time of his death he was the oldest magistrate, still being recorded with the Craven bench. He quickly became immersed in politics, as a Liberal, and was a prominent opponent of the Corn Laws. He was first elected to the House of Commons as the member for Clitheroe but was unseated when a petition was drawn up "owing to the indiscretion of an agent". In 1847 he was back in Parliament, being elected unopposed for Clitheroe. In 1852 Wilson was re-elected but, for a second time, was thrown out "for bribery or treating on the parts of his agents." So, the man whose primary claim to fame was to have been Skipton's first MP, was in fact twice thrown out of Parliament!

Wilson then became the Liberal MP for the northern division of the West Riding, covering a vast area including Skipton and, in 1885, upon the redistribution of seats, was unanimously adopted as the candidate for the new constituency of Skipton. The election was keenly fought against the Conservative candidate, SC Lister, and Wilson, by now a baronet and 82 years old, campaigned with vigour, taking the seat with 5,059 votes against 4,269.

Gladstone introduced a Home Rule Bill in the new Parliament which split the Liberal party, although Wilson remained firmly loyal to the Prime Minister. It seems as though he was keen to retire at the 1886 election called over Home Rule but was persuaded to defend his seat, opposed and defeated by the Unionist candidate Walter Morrison

HENRY ALCOCK

The Alcock family of solicitors were extremely powerful people in 19th century Skipton. For a start they owned extensive parts of the town and prospered on the rents. His two daughters were carried to school by sedan, a fact which appears to have been mocked by those in the town and they seemed to flaunt their wealth. It was Henry Alcock who built Aireville in 1836 and he seemed to serve on every local authority or committee of note.

When, in 1858, a Board of Health was formed for Skipton (a precursor of the council), Henry Alcock was its first chairman. In 1860 he was appointed to the Commission of the Peace for the West Riding. He was chairman of the Gas and Water Companies of Skipton, Chairman of the North Western Railway Company, Treasurer of the Poor Law Union of Skipton and Keighley (which ran the workhouses) and a trustee of the Skipton Building Society. He was also head of the flourishing Craven Bank of which his father had been the co-founder and acted for the grammar school in its previously chronicled dispute with headmaster Thomas Gartham. In short, this was not a man to mess around with. He was also instrumental in the financing of the new Christ Church in Skipton

Alcock was a solicitor whose firm eventually developed into Charlesworth, Wood and Brown which still thrives in the town today (his grandfather, John Alcock, was the founder of the firm, in 1732, and it was to have numerous partners during its existence). By 1853 it seems that Alcock's legal work was taking a back seat to his commercial interests. The Craven Bank, in particular, was thriving and in 1856 he retired completely from the legal firm, leaving his partner George Robinson in charge. Four years later he was struck off the Roll of Solicitors at his own request as he was becoming increasingly involved with his public duties.

By 1860 he was running the town in charge of the Local Board of Health which took charge of matters such as sanitation, health, roads and water supply but his health appears to have been deteriorating. After this date he spent his winters on the Continent and it was while at a health resort in Pau that he died of dropsy on December 23 1869.

The obituaries in the Pioneer were fulsome in their praise: "During his long and eventful professional career, Mr Alcock has occupied a prominent position and has always taken a foremost place among the gentry of the neighbourhood. Mr Alcock's character, both in public and private life, was one which had won for him the esteem and regard for all classes of society. As the owner of considerable house and other property in Skipton and elsewhere, Mr Alcock was a kind and indulgent landlord and held in great respect by his tenantry. His private charities, though unostentatious, were almost unbounded. Ample testimony could be given of his liberality in this respect and to the abundant store of provisions which has from time to time left the hospitable walls of Aireville to supply the wants of the poor and afflicted."

The Pioneer was to call for him to be remembered via a cattle trough and drinking fountain in the High Street but this idea never took off, although a reredos in Holy Trinity, erected at a cost of £1,000 given by his widow in 1874, is a permanent reminder of his power.

TOM CLARKE

TOM Clarke used his £180 demob money, a cash payment when leaving the services, to start what was to become a multi-million pound international concern – the Silentnight group.

Born in Skipton, Tom Clarke was an accomplished sportsman. He was regularly to be found in the foot races around the area. Just after the war Skipton races attracted crowds of several thousand when they started in 1946 on land off Carleton Road. His athletic prowess in these events helped subsidise the fledgling business.

During World War Two, Tom Clarke served in the Royal Navy on the hazardous Russian convoys which were prize targets for German U-boats and aircraft. His courage under fire earned him the Distinguished Service Medal, though he rarely spoke of it. On one occasion his ship came under fire from an enemy aircraft and all its deck gunners were shot. The commanding officer ordered the ship's signalmen to take up the guns and it was Tom Clarke who shot down the enemy plane.

Demobbed, he ploughed his £180 into setting up a business repairing worn-out mattresses, at first in the back yard of his home in Alma Terrace, just off Otley Street, Skipton. His wife Joan worked alongside him and together they were able to acquire small premises in Coach Street, Skipton. In those austere post-war times, new mattresses were almost impossible to obtain but the Clarkes ploughed any profits back into the company, becoming one of the first to import a tape edging machine, which allowed him to begin making mattresses and led to further expansion.

By 1949 the business had begun to outgrow the Coach Street premises and Mr Clarke began to look elsewhere in Skipton for larger premises and the financial backing to expand the business. However, he was turned down and he moved instead to Barnoldswick, where the mill industry was in decline and space was plentiful. There was also a pool of labour, former textile workers who were quick to pick up the bed making skills which have turned Silentnight into Britain's largest business of its kind, employing some 800 people. The failure of Skipton to back his business acumen was said to have sparked a resolve not to invest in the town, although he continued to live there.

A fire at Butts Mill nearly proved disastrous for the business but Tom and Joan Clarke overcame that and bought Moss Shed, where the Silentnight plant is still located, for £25,000. A double shift system brought in was a turning point in the company's fortunes. More factories were set up as the company split into divisions making other furniture to beds. Overseas factories were set up.

In 1973 Silentnight went public, making Tom Clarke a very wealthy man overnight but he kept his hands on the tiller. He was still at his desk long before many of his workforce started their shifts and stayed there until late. He had little time for trade unions and that led to a bitter strike early in the 1980s. Unwittingly he found himself caught up in the great trade union battles such as Grunwick and Wapping and Mrs Thatcher dubbed him "Mr Wonderful" when she opened the company's showroom at Salterforth. It was a description that came to haunt him during the lengthy strike.

In 1981 his services to British industry were recognised when he was awarded the OBE. The 1980s were one of continual expansion for Silentnight and the company was even to return to Skipton, opening the Pocket Spring Company on Airedale industrial estate, which manufactures beds of the highest quality. He contracted cancer and died in December 1993.

GEORGE LEATT

GEORGE Leatt was the son of a foundry worker at Varley's who went on to restore the old Corn Mill to working order. His first job was collecting the Telegraph and Argus from the railway station and rushing into town to sell them – the swiftest paperboy sold the most! At the age of 13 he joined the Co-op but his great love of breeding and showing dogs was to lead to a dispute with the manager. Apparently while a trip to football on a Saturday afternoon was a reasonable excuse for time off, heading for a dog show was not and so in 1944 George started work at Clayton's, the corn and seed merchants who had a large shop in Middle Row. Mr Clayton died in 1946 and George went into partnership with his daughter, Alice Simpson, buying her out in 1954.

Trade increased when the shop was moved to Albert Street into the former Ellesmere Press building but the lease expired and in 1979 the business was moved into the Corn Mill.

George had bought the old corn mill from a Mr Bramall in 1964 and the following year set about restoring and repairing two water wheels inside. The aim was to restore the mill more or less as it was in the early days and he turned it into a museum. During the 1974 miners' strike four hour blackouts were enforced plunging the town into darkness – except the mill. A turbine was used powered by the water wheels so that the mill was a blaze of light. The corn mill was back in production, grinding wheat to produce its own flour which was sold to the visitors.

During this time his reputation in the dog world grew. He exported dogs all over the world, bulldogs at first and then border terriers and went all over the country judging dogs. He was an international dog judge, qualified to judge 110 breeds. He died in 1985.

BILLY GELLING

A surviving picture of Billy Gelling shows a somewhat jaunty looking figure in a battered top hat with a twinkle in his eye. He was an instantly recognisable figure in Skipton between the two world wars, either in the pubs or pushing a cart through the streets with reclaimed coal. He was invariably dressed in top hat and waistcoat but no shirt.

The source of much of this coal was the canal and, in particular, where it joined Dewhurst's Mill by the Brewery Lane swingbridge. Here canal barges brought their supplies to power the looms of the mill and Gelling, armed with a bucket with holes in it on the end of a long pole, would scavenge for coal dropped by accident into the waters of the canal as it was loaded from the barge holds on to the wharf. And it appears that Gelling was such a character that the bargemen or Dewhurst's employees would "accidentally" slip a shovel load or two into the water for Gelling to retrieve. Indeed, there are suspicions that the very men who tipped it in would later buy it back at a much lower price than the going rate from Gelling as he wandered through town with his cart.

Gelling could neither read nor write but was taken to the town's heart as one of those "loveable rogues" in the Arthur Daley mould. Many a Skipton boy was told by a despairing mum that he "looked like Billy Gelling" as he came home after a day's play with shirt hanging out, trousers torn and liberal amounts of muck splattered over clothes, knees and face! Billy Gelling would have been amazed to find himself in a list of Skipton notables, but any older Skiptonians know him well!

THOMAS CRESAP

THE name Thomas Cresap may mean little to most Englishmen, or even locals, but for the students of the early, formative days of America he is a major figure. Born in Skipton, nothing is known of his early life, except that he left at the age of 15 to start a new life in the fledgling colony of America. He went on to lead a colourful career part pioneer like Davy Crockett part secret agent, speculator and farmer.

What is known is that he married a farmer's daughter, Hannah, from Baltimore County of Maryland in 1727-8 and ran into debt to the amount of £9, possibly from attempts to trade forcing him to spend a time in Virginia making enough to pay off his debts and return to Maryland.

At this time, probably due to his contacts with the powerful Washington family in Annapolis, then the principal city of Maryland, he appears to have become agent for the Calvert family, headed by Lord Baltimore, a position he held for at least the next four years and possibly for the next forty. In 1729, just one year after being broke, he bought a farm called Pleasant Garden deep into territory that had been disputed between the Penns of Pennsylvania, and the Calverts. Within the year he was also made a Justice of the Peace, and Captain of Militia.

At this time, all along the border zone between Pennsylvannia in the north and Maryland in the south there was a state of constant unrest and regular raids. The Penns claimed that the border should be 20 miles south of the recorded border at 40 degrees N. The squabbling along the border centred on the Skiptonian the Pennites called "The Maryland Monster", Thomas Cresap.

Farmer and magistrate Cresap became a focus for the Penn-initiated troubles. He was accused of (but the claims were never substantiated) killing Indians, wounding horses and generally being a pain in the backside. His home was attacked by gangs with musket fire and a native Indian was sent to kill him. The

Indian, rather than carry out his task actually warmed to Cresap and discloses the Pennite plot.

The Maryland Government stirred the cauldron a little by dispatching Captain Thomas Cresap JP with 20 armed men to construct a new river crossing ferry flat close to Pleasant Garden, in opposition to one close by operated by Penn. One night the Pennites crossed the Susquehanna River on their ferry hoping to catch Cresap unawares, but Hannah had been posted as lookout above the ferry and rode to Pleasant Garden to warn her husband and his supporters. During the ensuing fight one of the attackers was wounded and the fight is called off. The story goes that Pennites called on Hannah for a candle so that they might attend to their wounded friend. Hannah, whether expecting a ruse or simply matching her husband's belligerence, called back that she wouldn't send a candle and added she hoped they discover the wound to be in his heart!

The man, a Knowles Daunt, was in fact wounded in the thigh, but soon died of his wounds. The Pennites issued a warrant for murder, and Thomas was tried but found not guilty by the Maryland authorities, to the disgust of the Philadelphia Government and all Pennsylvania Colony.

More trouble followed when the High Sheriff of Lancaster County, Pa, tried to arrest a neighbour of Cresap called Jacob Loughman and delivered a severe beating to Loughman's wife. The sheriff was captured and hauled in front of the local magistrate - Thomas Cresap. Shortly after this, on November 24 1736, the Penns, probably as a result of the humiliation of being hauled in front of Magistrate Cresap, flipped into overdrive. They despatched another raiding party and this time successfully surprised the stockaded house. Plied with rum they demanded that Thomas surrender. In a later statement he said: "My answer was I would not surrender myself a prisoner to them, for that as I was in my own house, which I thought my castle. I have good cause and the Laws of England to protect me".

While Hannah escaped, Cresap was captured and bound and taken back across the river. In the darkness Cresap delivered a well-aimed elbow to his guard which toppled the unfortunate man into the river. High on adrenaline and fearing that their captive was escaping in the water, ferry poles were use to hit the splashing man "randum tandrum" until "poor Paddy – for he was an Irishman – not pleased with this sport made such lamentable cries that they discovered their mistake".

Aware now of the problems that faced them the guards then took Thomas to the blacksmith to have handcuffs fitted about his wrist. Mistaking his quietness for acquiescence they guarded him less closely, whereupon he smashed the manacles onto the head of the hapless blacksmith. He was then paraded by his captors through the streets of Philadelphi, capital city of Pennsylvania. A question called by one in the crowd "How do you like Philedelphia" was answered with "This is the finest city in the Province of Maryland".

There followed several weeks in prison for Thomas, charged again with the murder of Knowles Daunt, and during that time there were hot protestations between Maryland and Pennsylvania. The King in England was petitioned to put a final end to the long running legal disputes. Thomas, offered his freedom, refused, insisting his case be bought to the King's attention. This is probably at Lord Baltimore's behest as it amplified his own petitions to the King, and Thomas remained in prison a guest of the Pennsylvanians until the later summer.

After the king's comments on the boundaries, Thomas accepted release and around 1738 he acquired Long Meadow, Cumberland County, Maryland, and started farming and trading. Over the next few years he traded pelts from the local Indians and eventually made a large shipment back to England. The French Navy intervened and captured the cargo – Thomas was broke yet again. As before he did "a moonlight flit", this time taking Hannah and their children with him. The Cresap family headed deeper into the province of Maryland, dropping from sight and from official reports. When they next appeared in records, the Cresap family had settled land further west than any non-native before him, across many ridges of the folded mountains and across numerous rivers. This land is on the banks of the River Potomac. It is plausible that Thomas was still an agent for Annapolis, the Maryland capital, or directly to Lord Baltimore.

The position of his new land was strategic. It is on an ancient Indian trail used by tribal war bands from the six nations in the north. If the war parties were not too large Cresap would provision them and he acquired the Indian name Big Spoon.

Here Thomas built a fortified homestead and called this place Skipton. It may have reminded him of the topography of his hometown, or he may have seen the similarity that roads made both places so strategically vital. The Cresaps continued to be hungry for land and in the neighbourhood there was a Thrashfield and fields called Linton.

Skipton 2000

In 1749 The Ohio Company was formed by the English Government with a grant of 500,000 acres to exploit the lands drained by the Ohio River behind the mountains that trapped the English against the Atlantic. This would also thwart the ambitions of the French, who occupied Quebec and Louisiana, and who were soon to claim all the land between. Thomas Cresap, who, as a prominent man of the province, was asked to join the company as a member, was to make a road through the territory, constructing what is known as The National Pike. Through this gap – right past Thomas Cresap's family home called Skipton, poured the thousands that would open up The American West. It's possible that if he had failed then the French might well have captured and settled all of central and western America.

The French and Indian war did not go well at first and the English were forced on the retreat. Cresap and his sons were in the front line and waged a defensive war from a temporary base at Conocoheague. During one of these encounters his son Thomas jnr was killed. The retreat east continued and the Cresap household was practically alone holding west of the Blue Ridge. But the tide turned and the end of the war was signalled by the capture of Fort Duquense.

Thomas Cresap's later years did not see his viguor decrease. He continued to acquire land and agitated for Maryland's independence from Britain. Thomas may have come back to England to take instruction from Lord Baltimore when he was about seventy. He was told to investigate the Potomac River to find which branch was the longest, for a dispute with Virginia had broken out. There is speculation that he returned to visit his home town around 1765.

Widowed and remarried when we was 80, his next appearance came during the war of independence. His son, Michael Cresap, was appointed to lead a company of Rifles in the fight against England but he had returned from a visit to Kentucky in a weakened state and turned the role down. The threat from his by then blind father to take his place if he was to ill to go, forced him to accept the appointment, and he gathered the finest rifles in his area and marched, with other riflemen joining every day. He completed the 550 mile trip in 22 days with the First Company of Maryland Rifles. But the trip exhausted him and he died of a fever aged 33. Michael was given a hero's funeral in New York with great pomp, three battalions, an entire battalion of officers and a large assemblage of civilians following the cortege.

At 90 Thomas Cresap was still active and conceived a plan to explore west, right to the Pacific. Had he been capable he would have scored yet another notable first. Thomas Cresap lived until January 31 1787, aged about 92.

Today the Cresap Society of America which represents all descendants of Thomas Cresap claims 12,000 known descendants. In 1928 A presentation lecture was made in Skipton about Thomas Cresap. In 1932 a plaque was presented and displayed in the town Hall Entrance, today it has pride of place in the Skipton Museum. In the Second World War an American Liberty ship, built on a British design, was named Thomas Cresap. Yet Thomas Cresap, pioneer and secret agent, remained largely forgotten in Skipton, Yorkshire although there is a move to name the pocket park on Springs Canal by Coach Street in his memory as part of the Millennium Celebrations.

JOHN WILLIAM AND JESSIE BLOSSOM COULTHURST

IN 1947 this Gargrave couple established a charitable trust that has greatly benefited the citizens of Skipton and Gargrave. The family seat was at Gargrave House, and John William Coulthurst MA's parents had Streatham Lodge as their London seat until 1898. The family which traces its local history to at least 1606 in Bank Newton, had strong links to the church, including Vicar of Giggleswick, the practice of law at what was to become the Lincoln's Inn based Farrer & Co. and ultimately banking with family being senior partners of the prestigious London bank Coutts and Co.

The family throughout recent history has pulled together many of the other famous families we have recorded, for Henry Coulthurst, lord of the manor of Cold Coniston married Dorothy eldest daughter of John Wilson of Eshton Hall on 17 May 1701 (forebear to one Sir Mathew Wilson). John Nicholas Coulthurst married Catherine Mary, daughter of Stephen Tempest of Broughton on 25 July 1825, (the family who were founders of St Stephens and earlier they were listed at the honourable ending of the siege of Skipton Castle). Mrs Coulthurst who was awarded the OBE for services to charity, died in 1985 having gained her 87th year, her husband died in 1949 aged 87.

The Trust has supported a host of local charitable and good causes over the past 50 plus years; notably in Skipton the move of Skipton Museum to new location in 1974. It financed the rebinding of The Petyt Library. All sporting Skiptonians will know of the Coulthurst Craven Sports Centre at Sandylands. Sport has also benefited in Gargrave with grants to both cricket and soccer clubs.

Appendix 4: Names and numbers

Throughout the book I have identified shops and buildings by their occupants at the time of publication. However, as the High Street shop owners change frequently and very few buildings have any indication of their number, it has been decided to provide a list of the shops and indicate, where known, their previous owners and function. I acknowledge the work and help provided by Mrs Valentine Rowley in compiling the following list.

THE HIGH STREET (WEST SIDE)

2 Farmhouse Fare (pies, pork butchers)

4-6 David Goldie (country and outdoor clothing)

Mount Pleasant

8 Castle Café (tea rooms and restaurant)

10 Healthy Life (health food shop with vegetarian restaurant above)

12 Rayner (opticians)

14 Coffee and Cream (café)

16-22 The Black Horse (pub)

24 Wild's (bakers and café)

26 Slater's (electrical goods)

28-32 Skipton Library (NYCC)

34 Craven College

36 Next (fashion clothing)

38 Thorntons (confectioner's)

  above **Craven Herald** (newspaper office)

40 Dorothy Perkins (ladies fashions)

42 Greggs (bakers)

44 Just Jeans (jeans, clothing)

Bay Horse Yard

46 Yorkshire Bank

Sterling's Yard

48-50 Stead and Simpson (shoe shop)

52 Boots Opticians

54-56 Boots the Chemist

58 Xtras (perfumes and fashion accessories)

  above **Decked Out** (designer menswear)

60 Baker's Oven (bakers and café)

Halams Yard

THE HIGH STREET – MIDDLE ROW

62-64 Jumper (knitwear)

66 JT Lloyd's (perfumery)

68 Craven Tuck Box (confectionery, newsagents)

70 Mr Minit (shoe and leather repairs, keys cut)

72 Mellow Moments (candles, gifts)

74 Hamiltons (ladies' wear)

76 Recollections (gifts)

78 Just Books (discount books)

80 Clifford Benjamin (opticians)

82-84 Bradford and Bingley Building Society

86-90 Edinburgh Woollen Mill (knitwear)

    below **le Caveau** (restaurant)

Sheep Hill

Exchange Buildings & 100 National Westminster Bank

SHEEP STREET

2 Lunn Poly (travel agents)

4 New Look (teenage clothing)

6 Vacant

8 Hannam (jewellery)

10 WH Smith's (books, stationery)

12 Universal Booksale (discount books)

14-16 Greenwoods (men's wear)

18 Clinton Cards (greeting cards)

20 Mo's (ladies' fashions)

Archway through to Victoria Square

22 Max Spielman (photo processing)

24 Dixons (electrical goods)

26-28 Clarks (shoe shop)

30 Famous Army Stores (outside wear)

32 Dacre, Son and Hartley (estate agent)

34 Maple Leaf Images (photo processing)

Cooks Yard

36 Thomas's (fine jewellery & watches)

38 The Woolly Sheep Inn (pub)

40-42 Dolland and Aitchison (opticians)

44 Skipton Fashion Centre (jeans and leisure wear)

HIGH STREET (EAST SIDE)

1 Brought Estates (property management)

3 Walker Foster (solicitor)

5-11 Craven District Council (offices)

15 Savage Crangle (solicitors)

Craven District Council offices

Skipton Town Hall

> **Craven Museum**
>
> **Skipton Town Council Chambers**

Jerrys Croft

25 Claire Whitaker (chocolates)

27 Thresher (off licence)

29 Toyworld Toymaster (toy shop)

31-41 Rackhams (department store, House of Fraser group)

43-45 Althams (travel services)

Otley Street

Skipton 2000

47 Motor World (motor accessories)

49-51 Barclays Bank

53-55 H Samuel (jewellers)

Entrance to Craven Court

57 Burton (men's wear)

Kendalls Yard

59 Skipton Building Society

Providence Place

61 HSBC (bank)

63-65 Halifax (bank)

67 Abbey National (bank)

69 British Heart Foundation (charity shop)

71 Oxfam (charity shop)

73 Johnsons (dry cleaners)

HIGH STREET – CAROLINE SQUARE

75 Now demolished

77-79 Superdrug (toiletries)

81-83 Woolworths

85 Ponden Mill (fabrics)

87 Now gone

89 Lloyds TSB (bank)

91 Imperial Cancer Research (charity shop)

93 Craven Pharmacy (chemists)